Awaken
to the
Healer
Within

RICH WORK
with
ANN MARIE GROTH

ISBN 0-9648002-0-9
Published by

Asini Publishing
2042 Ryan Road
Mosinee, WI 54455

Cover Photo by
Margaret Jackson

Quotations and illustrations in the chapter "The Human Energy Field" are
reprinted from *Vibrational Medicine* by Dr. Richard Gerber, copyright 1988
Bear & Co., Inc., P.O. Box 2860, Santa Fe, NM 87504.

Printed in the United States by

MI**SS**ION
PO**SS**IBLE
Commercial
Printing

P.O. Box 1495
Sedona, AZ 86339

Dedicated to all the Angels in our lives —
seen and unseen.

Acknowledgments

We wish to acknowledge all of our Teachers, Guides and Angels who have been part of our journey to bring forth the simplicity of true healing. Our teachers have come in many forms: our children, our parents, our relationships, our friends and acquaintances. There have been many, too numerous to count. From our very soul we gratefully acknowledge each one by saying, "Thank you for the lessons and the love that we have shared."

Preface

Have you ever read a book on health or healing, and when you completed it, you thought, "All of this sounds interesting, but what do I do for *me?*" In these writings we will offer you not only a very broad and thorough understanding of the healing process, but a complete healing at a very deep level of your Being, should you choose to accept it.

The explanations are simple and the healing affirmations are in understandable language. It need not be made complicated; true healing never has been.

About the Authors

Rich believes that true healing must come from within. He has worked with hundreds in the United States and Canada who have manifested this level of healing into reality — physically, emotionally, spiritually, financially and socially. From mended souls to mended bodies, the testimonies are too numerous to mention.

Having explored health and wellness for more than twenty-five years, Rich is on the leading edge of taking the mystery out of disease and demonstrating the simplicity of healing.

Rich Work

Having conquered cancer, heart disease, mercury poisoning, chronic fatigue syndrome, malaria and asbestos poisoning, his pursuit of the healing arts has brought him into a greater awareness of an area of healing that is often overlooked and more often neglected, yet it has been available to us since the beginning of time.

Rich conducts lectures and *Reclaiming Your Mastery* workshops.

❖   ❖   ❖   ❖   ❖

Ann Marie believes that only love can heal. After battling multiple sclerosis for several years, she now enjoys total vibrant health. After years of intensive study in the alternative health areas of nutrition, biochemistry, herbology, homeopathy, Reiki, craniosacral therapy, orthobionomy, polarity therapy, etc., she put all of her knowledge and training together to form a simple and understandable philosophy of health and healing. Ann Marie's Synchronistic Attunements and the divinely inspired Harmonic Essences align

Ann Marie

the energy systems of the body, raising the amplitude and flow of the life-force energy system, thus releasing the body's innate ability to heal itself and restore the incredible inner power of the body to its perfected state of being.

Ann Marie conducts lectures and gives workshops on *Harmonic Vibrational Essences* and *Synchronistic Attunement.*

✧   ✧   ✧   ✧   ✧

In the business world Rich was an organizer who through necessity had to see the big picture. It was natural that when he was faced with extraordinary health challenges, his mind looked for the broadest perspective from which to view the human healing process and bring some kind of completion to the search for health that seems never-ending in our society.

Having studied various forms of healing techniques, Rich found many were teaching bits and pieces of healing and were thus working with bits and pieces.

In the business world it was Rich's responsibility to "put it all together." Everything had to have a beginning, a middle an end and a purpose. He felt that Healing also should have a beginning, a middle, an end and a purpose. It is time, he says, to put an end to making a career out of healing our Being.

It is time to **Awaken to the Healer Within.**

Poems by ann marie

All healing experiences within this book are true.
The names of the persons have been changed
to protect their privacy.

✧ ✧ ✧ ✧ ✧

Some of the writings in this book
have been written without punctuation
This free style of writing was done intentionally
to convey that these messages have no boundaries
to allow your imagination to grow
without limitations

Table of Contents

Index of Affirmations

Index of Illustrations

Discernment

Allow me to begin with a statement that I make at the beginning of my lectures and workshops.

If you do something because I suggest it, you have done it wrong. If you do something because your doctor suggests it, you have done it absolutely wrong. Yes, listen to your doctor, listen to Rich Work. Then do the most important thing of all. Read the material that is available, talk to the patients, and if it "feels" right — I did not say "thinks" right — if it *feels* right, then it is right for you. What is right for you may be wrong for the next person and could even be harmful for another. No two persons are the same. It is time that we get in touch with our intuitive feelings. Your intuitive feelings will always guide you in what is right for you in the moment.

It is not my intent that a person should accept everything simply because I say it. All truth is truth, but not all truth is *your* truth. If you are in the middle of an earthquake and the roof is falling on your head, your truth is, it's going to be a bad day. However, if you are basking in the sun, playing on the beach, your truth is, it's going to be a great day. If it feels right, be open to it. If it does not feel right, then it is not your truth in the moment. It is time for discernment.

Reclaiming Your Mastery

As a true healing unfolds, doorways open to a new consciousness: an awareness of our totality, the human expression and our purpose from a higher perspective. We have redefined the healer as the person that *desires* the healing. No one else is responsible for making that decision. Only you hold the key to your destiny.

Most of us have been raised in a society that was formed around co-dependent relationships. Those who have given their power to others, allowing others to be responsible for their welfare, whether it is government, society or specific individuals, have indeed formed a co-dependent relationship. They have surrendered their power, their free-will choice.

True empowerment is to reclaim your power and allow no one else to violate your free-will choice.

✧ ✧ ✧ ✧ ✧

As the darkened room gives way to the light of a single candle, so does fear give way to love.

There is much being said about love, yet most are still searching for that elusive emotion and have yet to define its meaning.

I am often reminded of the story of the well-intended grandmother who bought a bicycle and gave it as a gift to her grandson Johnny. It made her proud when she saw the look of surprise and delight on his face.

Then sometime later she visited the home of her grandchild and noticed that the bicycle was nowhere is sight. "Johnny," she asked, "where is your new bike?"

Johnny's eyes twinkled and his face beamed. "I gave it to my friend Tommy," he said with excitement.

The grandmother was shocked. "How could you do that? I gave that bicycle to you. I expected you to take care of it and use it for yourself."

The gift was given with conditional love. There were certain expectations and rules associated with it. Yet Johnny accepted the gift unconditionally. If it truly were a gift, then it now belonged to him to do anything he wished. It brought Johnny great joy to finally have something of value to express his feelings (his love) for his best friend Tommy.

✧ ✧ ✧ ✧ ✧

Too often we look outside of us for *love* — someone to love us — for we see ourself as incomplete. Something is missing; we are not whole. If we only had someone to love us, then we would be complete.

We have not yet given permission to accept ourselves — to love ourself. The love we seek is within. It has been there all along, waiting to be recognized.

Reclaiming your Mastery

is to stand in Unconditional Love:

a state of being without Judgment.

✧ ✧ ✧ ✧ ✧

Affirmation for Standing in My Truth

From the Divine Love that flows through my Being:
I give myself permission to be all that I AM,
to stand in my Truth
in Unconditional Love,
with no judgment of myself
or of others.
I honor all others for the journey they have chosen,
but I now choose to be the observer
and not a participator,
if that is what I choose in the moment.
So be it!

✦   ✦   ✦   ✦   ✦

To **Reclaim Your Mastery** is one thing,
To **Live Your Mastery** is another

It is time . . .

If I Had Only

When I was young and free and my imagination had no limits, I dreamed of changing the world. As I grew older and wiser, I discovered the world had not changed, so I shortened my sights somewhat and decided to change only my country.

As I grew into my twilight years, in one last desperate attempt I settled for changing only my family, those closest to me. But alas, they would have none of it.

And now as I lay on my deathbed, I suddenly realize: If I had only changed myself first, then by example I would have changed my family.

From their inspiration and encouragement, I would then have been able to better my country and — who knows? — I may have even changed the world.

These words were written on the tomb of an Anglican bishop (1100 A.D.) a the crypt at Westminster Abbey.

Perspective

If I were to address an audience on what it is like to give birth to a child, I would have one viewpoint. Those women in the audience who had given birth would have another viewpoint. The women who had never given birth would have yet another, and the men in the audience would have a completely different viewpoint.

Imagine that you are standing on a beach. As you look out from shore, all you can see is a vast expanse of water. You turn, then notice a lifeguard in the tower and you shout, "Tell me, what do you see from up there?"

The lifeguard replies, "I see a vast expanse of water and two ships on the horizon."

Then you spot a hot-air balloon overhead. Straining your voice, you call out, "Hey mister, what can you see from your balloon?"

The balloonist lets his eyes scan from his viewpoint, then shouts, "I can see a vast expanse of water, three ships, and land on the horizon."

Each person sees life from a different perspective. No two of us will see anything from quite the same viewpoint. Each has had a separate journey. No two have had quite the same experiences. Yet each of you will receive something of value from these writings, depending on your viewpoint.

There are very few on the Earth today who have mastered their existence. Many have read books and found a few answers. They have gone from grade school to college without understanding the basics of energy and the power of manifestation. Allow me to begin with a few basics.

All truth is truth, but not all truth is your truth.

Is This All There Is to Life?

One day as I sat in my office, a thought that had been nagging at me for some time once again preoccupied my mind. "Is this all there is to life? To be born, grow up, go to school, get a job, marry, raise your children, pay off the mortgage, retire, roll over and play dead?" The thought left me feeling incomplete. Who am I? How do I fit in the greater picture? Is there a purpose to my life? Am I just an accident that is here for a fleeting moment of cosmic time?"

Within days a series of events began to take place. It was as though someone were leaving a trail of candy for me to follow, picking up the pieces one at a time. I called them coincidences, and began logging them on my computer. As they began to accumulate, I thought, "This is not just coincidence; there is more to this than meets the eye."

I had been aware of stories of spiritual happenings over the years. Although I had never discounted their existence, I had not gone out of my way to pursue them.

✧   ✧   ✧   ✧   ✧

I met a lady of Indian (India) descent. I knew that her spiritual background also included the belief in reincarnation. Although I was vaguely aware of the concept, I had never given it any further thought. The lady explained that when the body dies, the soul still exists. Nothing is lost except the physical body the soul occupied. Eventually, the soul may choose to reincarnate in another physical experience. Like a tree shedding its leaves, it has not died but is preparing to be reborn into a new experience. Just as the tree grows with each experience, so does the soul.

The more I thought about what she had said, the more my life appeared to have a purpose. The very basis of science, I thought, is that you can neither create energy nor destroy it; you can only change its form. If this is true, then the soul has always been and will always be. The soul is eternal.

❖　❖　❖　❖　❖

A friend shared with me his understanding of reincarnation. "Our Higher Self," he explained, "is the sum total of all our incarnations. As a soul, we want to experience the many aspects of life that are available to us in the world we live in." I interrupted, "In other words, our Higher Self is like a recording artist who produces a record. A recording that includes a waltz, rock and roll, fox trot, polka, tango, and a spiritual song. Each is a separate expression of the artist, and the artist is the sum total of all his experiences."

My friend smiled. "That is the best description that I have heard," he replied. He then handed me a piece of notepaper and added, "You might find this book helpful."

I opened the note. "*Life Between Life*, by Joe Fisher and Joel Whitney," it read. I acquired a copy of the book and read intently about a psychiatrist who worked with hypnotic regression. During regression with his clients, he found that not only was he able to take them back into past lives, but into the soul experience between lifetimes. This opened an entirely new frontier in his research.

Today information regarding reincarnation is readily available, and hypnotic regression into past lives is quite common. A Gallup poll in 1982 indicated that 23% of Americans believed in reincarnation. Research in this field has opened the consciousness, and at this time more than two in three persons now accept the concept.

❖　❖　❖　❖　❖

I had tried for some time to meet with a doctor who had a mutual interest in an area of health I had been pursuing. He agreed to meet me in his office one Sunday afternoon. We talked for several hours, and during that time his conversation shifted to another subject. He told of having had a massive heart attack and collapsing on the sidewalk as he was about to enter his car. As others were frantically working over him, his soul separated from his body. He saw himself standing on the sidewalk, looking down at his body lying on the pavement. He watched as the ambulance arrived and the crew worked frantically with the lifeless form. At that time his spiritual Being raced upwards to a brilliant blue-white light. The farther he went, the faster he traveled and the greater the feeling of peace that came over him. Reaching the pinnacle of this shaft of light, he met his father, who had died sometime before.

His father advised him that he was not yet ready to leave the Earth. The doctor argued with his father for four days, pleading to stay. Repeatedly his father would say, "Your work is not finished. You must go back." After four days the doctor awakened in intensive care, where his mother had been sitting at his bedside during the entire time. Opening his eyes and seeing her, he said, "Mom, I've just been talking to Dad!" She smiled knowingly and replied, "Yes, I know. I've heard every word you've said." She had not heard her husband speak, only her son's side of the conversation.

I listened intently as the doctor related his experience. He then went on to say that he was studying with a select group in communicating on a higher level of consciousness, and he daily communicated with his eleven-year-old son telepathically, even when they were not in each other's physical presence. Sometimes this would take place while he was at the office and his son would be at home. His son happened to be present with us that Sunday afternoon. The doctor shifted his eyes toward the young lad and said, "Isn't that right, son?"

The boy, looking like any average eleven-year-old, shrugged his shoulders in acknowledgment and said, "Sure," as if to say, doesn't everyone do this?

✦　✦　✦　✦　✦

While attending a major convention, I decided to attend a workshop on communication by Dr. Ray Noran. After an hour of talking on the subject, he began a demonstration of psychic communication. He first put several strips of three-inch-wide adhesive tape over his eyes, then a solid leather blindfold followed by more tape. Looking something like a mummy, he asked two volunteers to stand behind him and hold any denomination of American bills in their hands so that no one other than they or the volunteer next to them could see it. Dr. Noran then proceeded to read the serial number of each bill without error.

Remaining blindfolded throughout the entire demonstration, he then had volunteers bring various items such as watches, billfolds and jewelry. Placing these objects in his hands one at a time, he told startling facts about the person from whom it had come, and each time the owner would acknowledge the accuracy of the information. These were not people who had been planted in the audience. Many of them I knew personally.

Next he asked for written questions from the audience. Along with thirty other people, I wrote down my own question. "Will my African film *CHOBE* be shown on TV?" Then as an afterthought, I added, "Cable TV." The note was folded twice, placed into a basket with the others, then dumped into a larger basket and shuffled. The basket was held before Dr. Noran. He removed his first selection and said, "I will call the first name of the person who has written the note. Please acknowledge your name." He held the folded note momentarily in his hand, then said, "Rich!"

"Yes," I replied.

"State your name," he instructed. I did. Then after a moment of thought, he said, "You are a creative individual. You have done something creative, something you want to share with a broad group of people. You have photographed and produced a film, which you want to put on TV." Then as an afterthought, he added, "Cable TV," in exactly the same thought sequence I had written it.

He then proceeded to answer the remaining messages unerringly, adding some unexpected personal comments for some individuals, which visibly shook them. He stated that he was communicating at the alpha-beta level, a level that we all experience about twice a day when we fall asleep and just before we awaken.

Incidentally, the fact that my note was the first he selected might just have been merely another "coincidence."

✧   ✧   ✧   ✧   ✧

The following day I related to a friend both the doctor's out-of-body experience and Dr. Noran's reading of my note. When I completed the story, he calmly looked at me and said, "Yes, I know. I also have separated from my body. I know exactly what you are talking about! During a college football game I was hit severely and was lying unconscious on the field. As others frantically worked over me, I separated from my body and followed beside them as they carried my body off on a stretcher. At that time I began traveling at an accelerated speed toward a brilliant blue-white light. It was exhilarating, beautiful, peaceful. I also did not want to return. It was two days before I returned to integrate with my body."

✧   ✧   ✧   ✧   ✧

Although I had known my friend for several years, he had never before shared that experience with me. I wondered how many others may have had experiences and chose not to talk about them, believing others might look at them in disbelief.

The more I remained open, the faster such experiences manifested for me. The things that happened, happened for a reason. I was looking for that reason. I now realize it was the beginning of opening many doorways to my knowledge about my spiritual self and my purpose for being. I had asked the question, "Is this all there is to life?" Then I stepped aside and *allowed* the universe to provide the answers. I no longer believe in coincidences. I believe that all things are in divine order. There are no mistakes.

There is an endless list of reading material available. I certainly have not discovered anything new. After all, our limited understanding of the universe barely gets us from cradle to grave. We claim to have a belief in what lies beyond our limited vision, but how many are truly willing to open their minds and look beyond physical reality? I choose to approach all things with an open mind. If it feels right, I remain open to it. If it does not feel right, I do not accept it.

All Truth is Truth, but not all Truth is your Truth

My Story

by rich

My interest in wellness began more than twenty-five years ago when my father was diagnosed as having terminal, inoperative prostate cancer during his medical checkup at a major hospital in southern California. They had prescribed a long series of cobalt (radiation) treatments. However, my mother was a registered nurse and was not satisfied with the answers she was receiving. They then decided to seek a second opinion from a friendly doctor knowledgeable about cancer.

He advised them, "If you repeat this, I could lose my license, but a friend of mine is going out of the country to use a program of alternative therapy and is doing great. I suggest you check with him." Later I discovered the doctors had told my father that he had less than two years to live. Had my parents not listened to their intuitive guidance, my father would certainly have taken the cobalt treatments and the rest would have been history.

As it was, he left the country to receive treatment, and in a short time his cancer was in total remission. He was encouraged by a friend to go to a clinic in the States and be reexamined "just for the record." This he did, and of course the doctor confirmed that he no longer had cancer. My father said, "Yes, I know," and proceeded to tell him why. The doctor's reaction was, "Not true. Your cancer went away due to spontaneous remission," and entered it as such in his medical records.

At that time my mother sent me some literature on the therapy my father had received. I promptly put it in the drawer of my bedside stand, since I really had no interest in it. After all, it was not *my* cancer, and it all sounded confusing. Six months later I found that I could not sleep one night, and began reading the material. The more I read, the more I wanted to read. It was then that I became determined to learn why my father and many of his fellow patients were responding so well to a treatment that the medical profession was determined to discredit as worthless.

While traveling with my father for his therapy, I took the opportunity to have a complete physical – and I was also diagnosed as having cancer. It was never a concern for me, as I knew exactly what I had to do. In a short period of time, it also was in remission.

In 1981 I had triple bypass surgery, which failed totally in less than thirty months. (The bypasses themselves also became blocked.) I have had chronic fatigue syndrome, mercury poisoning, candida, asbestos poisoning of the lungs, malaria, plus a few other problems, and had to seek my own answers. I have been the student as well as the teacher. This began my intensive study not only of cancer, but of all disease that afflicts modern man and the various therapies employed for healing, including orthodox (accepted medical practice), alternative (using holistic methods), and also spiritual approaches to healing.

I have found many people who are teaching bits and pieces of about healing; therefore I see many who are practicing healing in bits and pieces: for example, "Let's try this and if that doesn't work, let's try that. If that doesn't work, we'll send you to someone else."

✧   ✧   ✧   ✧   ✧

We live in a society where 85% of the population will experience heart disease. One in five suffer from arthritis. One in four have recognizable symptoms of amalgam (mercury) poisoning. One in three have candida (yeast infection). One in five are suffering from chronic pain. One in two will get cancer. Medical texts define an epidemic as a situation where one in a thousand experience similar symptoms. Yet we have come to believe that what we are experiencing is normal.

Modern medicine has made disease – and more importantly, the treatment of disease – so complicated that many health professionals no longer fully understand the science in which they are engaged. Healing, the process of returning to the state of health, need not be complicated or expensive.

For years, as National Sales Manager and Director of Training for a major corporation, it had been my responsibility to "put it all together." I believe that a healing also should have a beginning, a middle, an end, and a purpose.

We no longer have the luxury of spending weeks and months to effect a healing; time is moving much too fast. It is time to take the mystery out of disease and bring forth the simplicity of healing.

Let us not limit our vision as we explore the many aspects of who we are and what we are capable of accomplishing in the healing process. Healing is not difficult. It never has been. It is only our belief systems that limit what is possible.

All things are possible.

The Master said,

"If ye believe and doubt not, nothing shall be impossible to you."

The Most Powerful Energy in the Universe

Thought is the most powerful energy in the universe. It is the fabric from which all things are made. Thought is "living energy." Thought is prayer. It is for this reason that we choose prayer as the most powerful healing tool of all. We acknowledge the power of prayer, but often deny the power of thought. Our thoughts, our vows, our contracts, our agreements, are more binding than any rope that man has ever made. Thought is energy. Energy is vibration. Vibration resonates at a frequency.

Each thought/vibration/frequency will affect our Being in one way or another. It can enhance our life-force energy, deplete our life-force energy, or just be compatible. The vibration of every thought, no matter how insignificant, will resonate throughout every part of your Being. You are much more than you see in the mirror every morning when you get up. You are mind, body and spirit. You do not have a body here, a mind over there and a spirit somewhere else. Each is an integral part, an inseparable part, of every other aspect of your Being.

The vibration of every thought, no matter how insignificant,
will resonate throughout every part of your Being.

During a workshop I often ask, "Let me see a show of hands. How many of you do *not* have a mind?" Everyone will look at me intently, but not one hand ever goes up. "Now that everyone agrees they have a mind," I continue, "would someone be kind enough to tell me where the mind is?"

A long pause usually follows, with many considering for the first time, Where is my mind? Then perhaps one hand may go up, and the individual cautiously says, "In the brain?"

"No," I respond. "We now live in the age of the computer, and most of us have a basic understanding of computer language. The *brain* is our computer's hardware. *Thought* is its software. The brain only amplifies thought. It will do nothing until we feed information into it, and that information comes in the form of thought. Throughout creation, nothing has ever happened until it was first preceded by thought." You did not get up this morning, put on your clothes, eat your meals, or pick up this book without a thought process at one level of consciousness or another. It is by our thoughts that we have created our reality, and it is by our thoughts that we can change it.

Thought is living energy.

Thought is prayer.

Prayer is the most powerful healing tool of all.

Universal Laws

Imagine yourself getting into a basketball game without knowing the rules. There you are, standing in the middle of the floor and someone throws you this dumb ball. You don't know whether to throw it away, sit on it or eat it. It would be very confusing. Yet most people get into the game of life without knowing the rules. There are certain universal laws that govern us whether we are aware of them or not. Just because you are unaware of the law of gravity doesn't mean that when you sit under the apple tree, an apple won't fall on your head.

1: The Law of Magnetic Attraction. You attract to you that which you desire. You also attract to you that which you do *not* desire — if you focus on it. If you focus on disease, you will manifest more disease. If you focus on poverty, you will manifest more poverty. If you focus on the lack of love in your life, you will only manifest more lack. It is not possible to create love when you focus on fear. It is not possible to create prosperity when you focus on poverty. That is the Law of Magnetic Attraction.

2: The Law of Creative Manifestation. Now that you understand law number one, invoke law number two. Intentionally focus on that which you desire. And *do not* focus on that which you do not desire in your life. If you are in a room where others are engaged in a conversation about something that you do not desire, politely excuse yourself and leave. To remain in that energy will only attract more of it into your life.

3: The Law of Allowing. The most difficult law of all. Put your thoughts into universal consciousness, reinforced by desire. Then step aside and *allow* the universe to manifest it for you. If you are *hoping*, you are not *allowing*. If you have *expectations*, you are not *allowing*. If you have expectations, it is like saying, "Okay, God, this is what I want. Now let me tell you how to do it!" And God responds by saying, "For heaven sakes, get out of the way and let me do it for you." The more you *expect,* the more you *hope,* the more you *try* to manage or control, the more you will interfere and retard the manifesting of your desires. The Law of Allowing means just that. After all, the Master said, "Ask and ye shall receive." He didn't say, "Ask and we'll go have a committee meeting and take a vote on it."

Allow us to share some of our own personal manifestations.

The Automobile

A few years ago I was at a point in my life where, although I did not lack for anything, I did not have much left over on payday after expenses. I was driving an older-model car, and I knew in the near future that I might want to retire and devote my entire energies to the work that I am now engaged in. I thought, "It would be nice if I could have a new car bought and paid for before that time." Yet I did not have the resources to do so.

The only car that really caught my eye was the Ford Probe. Each time I saw one going down the road, I would do a double-take and say, "Wow!" I could feel the adrenalin increase and the excitement build as I looked on. "Wow, there goes another one!" No other car interested me, and each time I saw another Probe, it made my heart sing and I would come alive with emotion.

Over the past twenty years I have produced more than ninety films. I was a one-man production company, doing the filming, editing and scripting through the final production of the film. Many of these were industrial films for my company. One day I received a phone call at my office from the Director of a large association. He stated that he desired a film on a subject that was important to the membership of their organization. He said, "Rich, I've been getting quotes on the film, and do you know how much they want to make it?"

I smiled and replied, "Yes, it's expensive, isn't it?"

I could hear him take a deep breath. "Yes, I had no idea."

I added, "As much as $3000 a finished minute of film."

"And more," he responded.

After a brief conversation, I suggested, "Would you like me to give you a quote?"

Without hesitation he answered, "Please do. I've seen many of your films and I have always admired your work."

I offered him a deal he could not refuse. As time progressed, the director began to appreciate the amount of work that goes into the production of a 30-minute film. Two hundred eighty hours later, working outside of my normal working hours, it was complete. Very pleased with the finished product, I handed him a bill for my labors. The director glanced at the invoice and said, "Rich, you have worked very hard to complete this film," then pulled his checkbook from the desk drawer, wrote out a check and handed it to me. To my surprise, he had made the check out for considerably more than I had asked for. He smiled. I gratefully accepted his gift.

The next day I went to the Ford dealer, ordered my Probe and wrote out a check, paid in full.

I had been so focused in the drama of this event that I did not realize until later that it was I who manifested my new car.

The Vacation

For weeks Ann Marie and I had not had a day off from our workshops and appointments. Feeling stressed from our schedule, we agreed that we needed to take some time off for ourselves and go play. Ann Marie said that she had never been on a houseboat, and that was one thing she would really enjoy. Two days later we met a friend in a restaurant, and during the conversation she mentioned that there was an opening for only two more people for an extended weekend on a houseboat trip on beautiful Lake Powell, Arizona. Would we be interested?

In unison we replied, "Yes."

The Camera

With all the film work that I have done, for years I saw the world through the lens of a camera. I have moved into a new life, and have sold my cameras and filmmaking equipment, keeping only one 35mm camera with interchangeable lenses. Even then I found this bulky and inconvenient to carry with me. As we traveled around Lake Powell, we were exposed to one incredible scenic view after another. Ann Marie said, "What we need is one of those new compact point-and-shoot cameras that will fit into my purse. Look at the beautiful country around us, and we don't have a camera." She then began asking everyone on the boat what kind of a camera they had, how much it cost, and how pleased they were with it.

Two days later our friend approached us on the houseboat and said, "I lost my camera some time ago and filed an insurance claim. After I had purchased another camera, I found my other one. I have no need for two cameras. Would you please accept this one as my gift?"

The Stage Play

A few days later we traveled to Salt Lake City and spent several days with some wonderful people. During this time Ann Marie overheard one of the ladies mention that she was going to a stage play with some friends. She turned to me and whispered, "I've never been to a professional stage play."

"Would that bring you joy?" I asked.

"Yes," she said excitedly.

Smiling, I looked at her and said, "Then it will happen."

Nothing more was said on the subject until the next day when the lady approached us and said, "I seem to have two extra tickets to the stage play tomorrow night. Would you like to come as my guests?"

It was a wonderful night and the play was outstanding.

The College Education

When Ann Marie was young, she always knew that she would grow up and go to college. There was no question in her mind. It was simply a *knowing* inside of her. Yet her parents' income was modest and did not reflect the ability to support her dream.

At the age of twelve, Ann Marie was in the car with her father, her brother and three other schoolchildren. Her father peered around the partially blinded inter section and carefully eased the vehicle out to cross the highway. He could not see the oncoming auto that had been clocked traveling at 90 miles per hour, and the driver of that auto, blinded by the sun, never saw them. They were struck broadside with such impact that it propelled Ann Marie's family car into the air, shearing off a telephone pole ten feet above the ground. The door next to Ann Marie was open, yet not one of the passengers were thrown out of the car. More incredible was the fact that no one in either car was killed. The accident left Ann Marie with her left elbow completely crushed and the possibility of a crippled left arm.

The insurance claim for Ann Marie's injury would take four years to settle, and the amount of the claim would be more than enough to see her through college, with some to spare.

The healing work that she has done since that time has almost restored the elbow, and she has complete use of the arm.

Manifesting Money

A close friend of ours required more money to complete a project that was very important to her and that would have a lasting, positive impact on the community, but she could not determine how she would get it.

All she knew was that her project had become a burning passion that must be completed. She owned an old van that did not run and was not worth the cost to repair. There was not even enough money to hire someone to tow it away. Then late one evening, an auto with several young people crashed into her van, totally demolishing it. Their insurance company gave her a check for the van, and in addition they hauled it away at their expense. The check was just enough to allow her to complete her project.

✧　✧　✧　✧　✧

Many people look upon such events as these and think, just another coincidence. But life has taught me otherwise. It is by this same Law of Magnetic Attraction that we manifest everything into our life.

Thought is powerful. Words are the extension of thought. Regardless whether it is expressed in the mind, as the written word, or as the spoken word, the power of thought is the same in all dimensions.

Thought can either create or destroy. You may know of someone who always seems to focus on the negative side of life. Have you noticed that the person always seems to attract those things that are negative? Think for a moment of all the destructive phrases that you have heard or that you may have even said yourself. Let me share with you a few that I have heard recently.

> He is a *pain* in the neck (and other bodily parts).
> I must have been *blind* not to have seen that.
> I lost my keys again; I must be going *crazy*.
> I bet this will *cost me an arm and a leg*.
> I would *give my left arm* if only I could . . .
> I'm *dying* to see what happens next.
> I'm so *sick* of this job I could just *die*.
> I was feeling better, but I got over it.
> Sometimes I wish I were *dead*.
> It just *kills* me to tell you this.
> This just tickles me to *death*.
> I must be *losing my mind*.
> This just makes me *sick*.
> I'm *dying* to tell you this.
> That makes me so *sad*.
> I got some time to *kill*.
> Oh, my *aching back*.
> Over my *dead body*.
> I could just *die* for it.
> Life sure is *hell*.
> I feel so *dumb*.
> I feel like ____! ·

Many of these phrases are repeated time and again through habit.

Remember, every one of your 100 trillion cells has a mind, a body and a soul. Your body is listening, and it understands your every thought. It responds to your every command.

A Message on Energy

Imagine the water pipes in your home. You know that there is water in the pipes at all times, yet no water will come forth until you turn on the faucet. Now let's apply this same thought process to the electricity in your home. The electrical current is always present in the wiring, yet you are unable to operate your lights until you complete the circuit. Electricity comes from the power pole into the wiring in your home or business, and completes the circuit by returning to the power pole. You can interrupt this flow of electricity by turning the switch to "off." The electricity is still there, but will not be activated until you flip on the switch and it can continue its path back to its source and complete the circuit.

Now let's look at this from another perspective. Energy cannot work for you until you complete the cycle of energy. It is a universal truth. Since everything in the universe is electromagnetic energy, it works on this principle.

Sending energy to others can work only if they are open to receive it and are returning energy to you in turn. If they are not returning energy to you, the flow of energy is interrupted and ineffective. This same principle applies to those who choose to "fix" others. Until a person has opened his "switch" to receive, the cycle of energy cannot be completed.

Let's take this one step further: Money is energy. Remember, everything is electromagnetic energy, and money is nothing more or less than energy. If you offer something of value, whether it be therapy, services or goods, the cycle is not completed until the other party exchanges something of value to complete the flow of energy. It can be in the form of monetary value, goods or services. It is then that the full value of what you have offered is received in full. They have made a commitment to receive.

Those who choose to see healing as a gift (regardless of its form) and choose to give it away are under an illusion. An energy exchange has not taken place. The switch has not been turned on. The flow of energy has stopped. True healing allows people to become an active participant in their own healing. When you have empowered your clients, you have truly given them a gift. Anything less is "fixing." You cannot fix the world. You can only assist, and you can only assist when you are asked to do so.

What I have just shared has been told many times in many forms. One that you may remember is the Japanese doctor who desired to find a more effective way of healing. He received his spiritual message to go sit on the side of a mountain and meditate for twenty-one days and the answers would be given to him. He placed a pile of twenty-one stones beside him and each day he would remove a stone. Finally, sitting on the mountain on a dark, moonless night with only one stone remaining, a brilliant light appeared in the distance and raced toward him from the sky, striking him in the forehead. Messages and symbols were burned into his mind. With this information, he rushed to the city and into the ghettos, healing the beggars and anyone he could find. He did not charge a fee, for after all, this was a gift from God. Much to his disappointment, he soon found the beggars had returned to their chosen livelihood, and no one had retained the gift he had offered.

They had not asked to be healed. They had not offered an exchange of energy. The switch had not been turned on. The doctor then decided to do what doctors have always done. He returned to his office, waited for others to come to him, and he charged for his services. It was then that his clients accepted and received their healing through the new healing modality that he had received. He called his gift *Reiki* (the Universal energies of Love).

The Japanese doctor had found that the gift he offered was effective only when there was an exchange of energy. The exchange of energy was a client's commitment to participate, which opened him to his empowerment. He thereby became willing to be an active participant in his own healing.

Ours Is a World of Energy

Science understands that there is but a single source of energy from which all frequencies emanate. Some call it life-force energy. Some call it universal energy. Some just call it the God force. They also agree that you can neither create energy nor destroy it; you can only change its form. Science also agrees that everything in the universe is electromagnetic energy. Everything you can see and perceive is energy — the birds, the bees, the grass, the trees, and you and me. Every cell in your body is electromagnetic energy. Every organ in your body has a frequency different from every other organ in your body. Your eyes work electrically, as do your brain, your muscles, your cells — and yes, even your thoughts and emotions are electromagnetic energy.

We know that there are herbs that enhance your heart and herbs that enhance your liver and so on. Although our logical mind has been trained to see herbs as a substance, our body recognizes them only as energy that will either enhance it, deplete it, or simply be compatible with it. As an example, when the liver is in a weakened state, its frequency has become distorted and in disharmony. To correct this situation and strengthen the liver, all we need to do is bring a powerful positive frequency into the body that will enhance the liver, thus bringing the liver back into harmony. That frequency could be in the form of an herb, or just the pure energy of a frequency that will enhance that part of the body.

I was involved in a demonstration in which the instructor asked all 120 persons in the room to hum a note, any note, and continue to hold that note until he told us otherwise. It was the most awful cacaphony of sounds you have ever heard, everyone sounding a different note. The instructor then took the microphone and began humming his own note very loudly and firmly. Within a few seconds, much to our a amazement, we found that without being aware of it, we were all humming in tune with the instructor. The instructor, having the more powerful note, drew everyone else into harmony with his frequency.

The strongest frequency always wins

The strongest frequency is LOVE

Everything you can see and perceive is energy. Everything has a frequency. We tend to see objects as matter; therefore we acknowledge their existence. Just because we cannot see something does not mean that it does not exist. Have you ever seen air? You have seen the effects of air. It can support a huge aircraft in the sky, and when moving rapidly, it can blow a house down. Air has a tremendous effect on our lives, and yet it is not visible as you look across the room, to the horizon, or at the stars on a clear night.

We perceive sound as frequencies picked up by our ears and relayed to our brain. If you were going to buy a new stereo system, you would travel to your favorite audio store and look at the specifications of their stereo systems until you found one with a range of 20 to 20,000 Hz (frequencies per second). This allows you to hear the clear high tones and those booming low bass sounds. This is also the approximate audible range of the human ear. Yet we are aware that there are sounds that vibrate outside of our audible range. There are whistles that emit sounds that dogs can hear but we cannot. Just because we cannot hear certain sounds does not mean they do not exist. It simply means that it is beyond the limited range of the human ear.

The same is true for our eyes. We see those things that vibrate in the limited range of frequencies our eyes are capable of receiving. We are unable to see those frequencies that fall outside of this range.

Our world is one of energy. Science already understands this. Now it is time that we become aware of the world that we live in.

There are many ways to demonstrate energy and how our body responds to various energies. Some are frowned upon by medical science, but this does not make them less valid, and tens of thousands of health practitioners around the world use them to validate their work with their clients. It is science of another type — the science of energy.

Ours is a World of Energy

Kinesiology

Kinesiology is the practice of muscle testing.

Science agrees that everything in the universe is electromagnetic energy. It is the very foundation of science. Everything you can see and perceive is energy. The art of muscle testing known as kinesiology makes it possible to test the human body's response to anything you can see and perceive.

Place your finger on the base of your throat. Now move your finger down about two or three inches onto the breastbone. It is at this point, behind the breastbone, that your thymus gland is located. Your thymus gland is the gateway to your immune system. Energy that affects your thymus gland in a *positive* manner will allow you to lock your motor muscles. A motor muscle is any joint muscle. It can be your shoulder, elbow, finger, hip, knee, etc. Any energy that affects your thymus gland in a *negative* manner results in the motor muscle becoming weak and unable to lock. Any energy that affects your thymus gland in a positive manner results in the motor muscle remaining strong. Although it is possible to demonstrate with any of the parts of the body mentioned, I usually prefer to use the shoulder muscle.

Since muscle testing is working with energy, it is important that you understand that your own thoughts are energy. It is possible to transfer your own thoughts (psychic energy) to the person you are testing. If the person doing the testing is not in complete integrity, the results can be affected. It is my suggestion that before you demonstrate this or any other form of energy work, you make a short affirmation.

Kinesiology done with integrity can be very accurate. It is only as good as the integrity of the person using it.

I will accept only those answers
that come from the highest source of the person
I am working with.

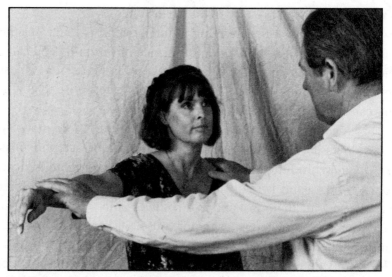

**Before muscle testing for anything, always test your subjects first
for their normal strength so that you will have a reference to the
level of their resistance.**

Have a willing volunteer stand facing you. Ask her to remove
any metal-rimmed glasses, watches and bracelets that are not completely connected in a circular fashion (the split type of bracelet you
can slip over your arm rather than over your hand) as well as any
heavy necklaces, including crystals – any objects around the wrist,
neck or face that may interfere with the test.

Ask her to hold her stronger arm straight out to the side parallel
to the floor, and resist the downward pressure that you will be
applying just above her wrist. You might ask her to "show me your
strength." Using two fingers (not your entire hand), press downward on her arm in a firm but not forceful motion. (Note: If a small
person is working with a large, muscular person, you may need to

use three or four fingers.) Do not use such pressure that you force the person's arm downward. You are not intending to arm-wrestle, but simply to test normal strength. Feel that strength. Feel the resistance.

When something is placed within a person's energy field, it is possible with kinesiology to test whether it will enhance that person's strength or deplete it. This is done by placing the test substance in the opposite hand of the one you are testing. Another method is to have the subject hold the material on the bare skin over their thymus while testing. You might want to try placing some sugar in a transparent sandwich bag. Now apply the same pressure as before. You will find that person's strength has been greatly reduced; the motor muscle will not lock and will be unable to resist the pressure of your two fingers.

Try salt. Most persons will test weak. It is important to understand what your body is telling you. If you test strong, your body is saying, "I'll take more of this; it gives me strength." If you test weak, it is saying, "Don't give me this; it weakens my immune system." We know that the body needs sodium. However, in our Western diet, we get an overabundance of salt in the processed foods we eat, so the body is saying, "I already have more salt than I need,

Motor muscle will not lock; it is unable to resist downward pressure.

and any more will only deplete my system."

Now take a battery-operated wristwatch (if you have one) and place the face of the watch into the palm your subject's other hand, closing the fingers so that they touch the back of the watch. Now repeat the arm test. The person will usually test weak. The battery in the watch emits one pulse of energy per second, going directly into the body's electrical system, creating a short-circuit and weakening the immune system. Anything that weakens your immune system allows you to become more susceptible to illness. (Please don't throw your watch away; there is a way to protect yourself from this energy, which we will address later.) You will test strong with the standard spring-loaded, wind-up watch (without a battery).

If your subjects wear metal-rimmed glasses, test for their normal strength without glasses, then ask them to put their glasses back on. Test again and you will find they will test weak. The reason? Our brain has two lobes, one side to create and the other to store information. The brain works electrically, so energy coming from the body enters the metal earpiece and travels the path of least resistance, following the metal frame to the other side of the head. Energy wants to complete a circuit and will always attempt to find a path if one is present. In this case, it now enters the opposite side of the head, traveling through the body to the metal on the other side. Interestingly, if you attach a metal chain (an accessory for glasses) to both earpieces, the energy will follow the path of least resistance, in a necklace effect, and the person will test strong. You can have a lot of fun at your next house party demonstrating how the energy of different substances or thoughts affect your strength and your immune system.

As we have already established, everything in the universe is energy and has a specific frequency; therefore anything you can see and perceive can be tested in this manner. Let us take this a step further.

Test your subjects for their normal strength. Ask them to repeat the following words one at a time, testing their strength after each word: insurance; doctor; hospital. You will find that each of these words will cause weakness. Ask them, "What do each of these words mean to you?"

Most often the answers are, "Insurance is something I buy because I'm *afraid* I will have an occasion to use it. A doctor is who you go to when you are *sick*. A hospital is where you go when you are *really sick*." Each one of these words registers in the subconscious mind as a negative word; therefore you test weak.

Ask your subjects to say the word "healthy." Much to their surprise, most people will test weak. "Healthy" is a state of transition, moving from a state of illness to where they would like to be. Now ask them to say the word "health." They will test strong. Health is the goal you wish to achieve. The lesson is simple: The Law of Magnetic Attraction says that you attract to you that which you focus upon. Therefore, if you focus on your disease, you will always be in the state of disease. If you focus on the process of getting well, you will always be in the *process*. Ask your subjects to say the word "perfection." You will find that they are very strong. Perfection *is* the goal, the state of being that most people wish to be in. Many hospitals and clinics are now working with, and instructing their patients in, positive thinking and visualization. When you focus on your perfection, your total being must respond to the Law of Magnetic Attraction and will gravitate to that which you focus upon.

Henry Ford once said, "Everyone has two choices in life: (1) you can do it; or (2) you cannot do it. In either case you are absolutely right." Ask your subjects to hold their arm up and say, "I cannot do it." They will be weak. Then ask them to say, "I can do it." They will test strong. In either case, they are absolutely right.

Every vibration in the universe that we see and perceive is registered in our energy field, in our subconscious mind – light, sound, color, clothing, plants, trees, air, metals, and materials of all descriptions. The very air you breathe, the foods you eat and the water you drink is energy. It is the fuel that your body runs on. Thought is energy. Every thought that enters your consciousness or subconscious is recorded instantly and has an impact on you in one manner or another. Negative thought will deplete your life-force energy.

Positive thought will enhance it.

Ask your subjects to say the word "fear." They will test weak. Now say "love." They will test strong, very strong. Love is the most powerful positive vibration in the universe. It is love that heals and fear that destroys.

Have you ever taken a photograph? Did you ever question how the image got onto that piece of paper in the camera? Do you suppose the folks at Kodak are scratching their heads and saying, "How do you suppose that happened?" I don't believe so. They know that each color has a frequency different from every other color. They know how to coat film with highly sensitive chemicals that each react to a specific range of frequencies. Frequencies from the birds, the bees, the grass and the trees travel through the lens onto the film in a fraction of a second, and a photograph is born.

The same thing happens to our eyes. Simply looking at something that is positive energy for you will make you strong. The opposite is true for something that has a negative effect on you. Try muscle testing while you are looking at a beautiful flower. Try again while looking at a photo of a toxic waste dump. Try looking at the beautiful sky, then again while looking at the fluorescent lights in an office. Try testing as you look at someone you love, then again while looking into the screen of your television set.

Now walk as far away as you can from your television, look directly into the screen and test again. You will still test weak. The electromagnetic energies travel to you just as the energies of your eyes travel to the television. For electricity to work, it must complete a circuit. Not only are all of us energy receivers, we are also energy transmitters. Our energy affects everyone around us in one form or another.

Your body is surrounded by an energy field. It is the energy field that is called an aura. This energy has been well-documented, and by using special photographic equipment, you can take black-and-white or colored photos of the aura. This is known as Kirlian photography. Those knowledgeable in martial arts are well aware of the energy fields and meridians surrounding the body. Have you ever noticed the hand movements of those martial artists as they approach their opponent? They are not moving their hands just to be polite, but to center their own energies and disrupt the energies of their opponent.

After muscle testing for strength, simply sweep your hand down the front of the body of your subjects (do not touch them). Test again and they will be weak. You have disrupted their energy meridians. Now reverse this process by placing your hand near their knees and quickly raising it up and past their head in one smooth motion. Your subjects will now test strong. You have realigned their energy meridians. Now, standing in front of them, make a large Z with your hand in front of their body with a firm and forceful motion. Test again and they will be weak. You have interrupted their energy meridians. Now complete your work by moving your hand quickly up in front of your subjects to once again realign their meridians.

Kinesiology is a wonderful, entertaining way of demonstrating the effects of energies. However, unless you are a licensed medical practitioner, kinesiology should never be used for the purpose of diagnosing someone else.

There are many interesting books that are available on the subject of kinesiology. *Your Body Doesn't Lie* by Dr. John Diamond is a most appropriate title, because your body is incapable of lying. It will always tell you what will enhance or deplete your life-force energy.

Dowsing

Dowsing, like kinesiology, is another way of using energy to obtain answers to questions. It is possible to test virtually anything you can see and perceive. You may be familiar with dowsing for water, or water witching. As a boy, I remember when my grandfather hired a man to come to the farm and find the most likely place to dig a well. Using a branch from a tree that looked much like the wishbone of a chicken, he held the two ends of the Y in his hands and pointed the other end forward. He walked around the property until the branch suddenly began to vibrate and was finally pulled downward. The man said, "This would be a good choice for your well."

You may have seen a serviceman from the gas or telephone company walking across your yard with a couple of metal rods, trying to locate where the pipes or cables were buried. There are dowsing associations throughout the world that meet to share their discoveries, both old and new. I demonstrate with dowsing rods to open people's awareness of how energy works. As with all forms of working with energy, integrity is absolutely essential.

Dowsing rods can be made from two 36-inch welding rods, which can be obtained from your local welding supply dealer or a builders supply. Copper-coated steel works very well, but you may also use copper, stainless steel — or simply straighten out a couple of heavy metal coat hangers (unpainted is best). Make a 90-degree bend about six inches from the end to form a handle. Your new dowsing rods can now be used to find anything you energize them for.

Take a coin (a quarter works well) and while holding the two rods in one hand with the long ends pointing downward, place the quarter in the other hand and rub the coin against the length of the rod and toward the floor. You have just energized the rods to the vibration of the alloy within the coin, and they will now find that

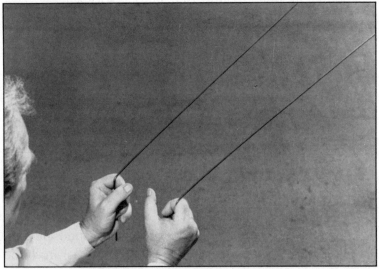

Holding two rods in a normal position.

alloy or coin. Throw the coin on the floor a short distance from you. Holding the rods by the handle, keep the rods horizontal and parallel to each other, about 9 to 12 inches apart. Now walk slowly toward the coin. As the rods start to pass over the coin, they will begin to cross when they are directly over it, indicating its location. The interesting thing is, although the coin could be under the rug or buried in the ground like the buried cable the telephone man was looking for, the rods will nevertheless cross, indicating where the material is. Try this exercise using different materials such as cloth, wood, a potato, etc.

Ask your subject to stand up: then, using only one rod, wipe the rod down with her hand two or three times. Hold the single rod pointing directly at your subject with the tip 6 to 12 inches away. Ask her to start walking slowly around you, watching the rod as she walks. (If you are holding the rod in your right hand, ask her to move to your left, and if the rod is in your left hand, to move to the right.) The rod, being energized for a specific person, will follow that person like a magnet.

Now ask your subject to return to her original position next to you. Hand her a note with the words, "God, I am the ultimate Healer" written on it. Ask her to read it silently three times, then drop

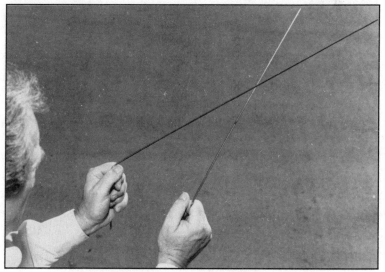

Rods cross, indicating location of object searched for.

the note onto the floor. Point the rod toward your subject once again, ask her to move slowly, as she did before, watching the rod. This time, much to her surprise, the rod will not follow. The reason? The word "God" vibrates at a frequency of 186 billion cycles per second. Each time you repeat the word "God," you raise your own vibrations to a higher frequency. Simply saying "God" three times (in love) changes your frequency such that the rods no longer recognize you. Now ask your subject to wipe the rod one more time, then repeat the demonstration. The rod will now quickly respond and follow the higher vibration of the person to which it has been energized.

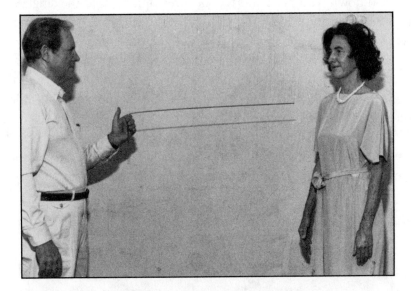

Again ask the subject to wipe the single rod down three times, each time repeating aloud, "It will not work, it will not work, it will not work." Point the rod toward the person as before and ask her to move slowly. The rod will not follow. You have just demonstrated that there is *no frequency in negative thought.* I did not say negative energy; I said "negative thought." If you believe it *can't* be done, it *will not* be done. If you believe it is *not* possible, it *will not* be possible.

There is no frequency (energy) in negative thought!

If there is no frequency (energy) in negative thought, why do people get disease? Here we must redefine the term "negative thought." Disease occurs when a person has a depleted immune system. Disease may not be desirable, *but it is not a negative thought.*

Negative thought is a belief system. It was "known" for many years that humans could not run the measured mile in less than four minutes, and thus no one did. Then a young Englishman named Roger Bannister ran the mile in less than four minutes, and in that moment changed the consciousness of the world. Someone had forgotten to tell him that it couldn't be done. Today if you are unable to run the mile in less than four minutes, you probably will not be invited to the Olympics.

All your life you have been told of all the things that you cannot do. Now I am going to suggest that you can do *all* things.

Positive thought is also a belief system. If you believe that something is possible, then it *is* possible. As we move forward in our journey in this writing, we will demonstrate that

All things are possible.

Does God Really Exist?

Life is a series of lessons. We grow not only from our own experiences, but from the experiences of others.

Frederick Merat is a sincere individual who has devoted his life to assisting others. His many talents have yet to be discovered by the world. Frederick's life journey is one that would fill a book, and it is his intent to do so. The following is but one chapter from his life, as told by Frederick.

Does God Really Exist?

I have been having a love affair with God since my fifteenth birthday. Never once did I deviate from that path. No matter how high I rose or how low I fell, not once did I forget my purpose for being here. I have been on an incredible learning adventure that has brought me to where I am today and it has prepared me for the new adventure that I am now beginning.

When I was fifteen, I had suffered an emotional experience that launched me into a state of deep depression and withdrawal. While in that state, I began to hear a voice inside my head. It kept repeating over and over the words, "Trust me, believe in me, and I will give you strength and knowledge to sustain you through all that you shall endure." I kept hearing this voice for about a week. I began to think I was going crazy, so I told this voice to go away, to leave me alone. After several days, it said, "Very well, I will go. But if you ever need me, just call, and I will be there."

I knew this voice to be that of God, and I knew even then that It was calling me to serve. But I must tell you, there probably is not a greater Doubting Thomas living than I.

So instead of going along with the flow, I challenged God to prove to me that It existed. It responded by giving me several miraculous signs and by creating an abundance of situations and events that could not be explained in any terms other than miracles. But I still chose to ignore Its gentle and loving communication, Its gentle way of calling me to serve.

So I issued a second challenge to God. This time I said that there was only one way that God could prove to me that It existed. It would have to bring me to my knees. And if It harmed one hair on the head of anyone I loved while doing it, I would spend the rest of my life destroying the belief in It. How foolish of me! I had no idea what I was asking for when I uttered these words. Perhaps it was the Doubting Thomas in me that questioned the existence of God.

It did not take God very long to respond. One week after I had spoken these words, my wife and I left Ohio to drive out to California to pick up my wife's sister and newborn baby, and bring them back to their parents' home in Pennsylvania.

It was early March in 1968, spring was on its way, and the weather was beautiful. Not a cloud in the sky, no snow on the ground. It should have been clear sailing all the way.

Not so. We had just dropped our children off at my wife's parents and were on our way. Within fifteen minutes we ran into a blizzard that came out of nowhere. We had to drive all the way to Columbus traveling no faster than fifteen miles per hour. In Columbus we were in a twelve-car accident, being hit from the side by a car and from the rear by a truck, which spun us into the guard rail. No one in the twelve cars was hurt in any way, not even a scratch.

We continued on. During this adventure we had to replace six tires that mysteriously developed huge bubbles in them that could have exploded at any moment during our high-speed travels. At two o'clock in the morning, while traveling at sixty miles per hour in the open farmlands of Oklahoma, we hit a horse that was standing in the middle of the road, killing it and demolishing the front windshield. Glass was everywhere, but neither my wife nor I were hurt. Not even a scratch.

This was also my first of many UFO encounters. For nearly two hours before we had the accident with the horse, there was an unknown aircraft with blinking colored lights far off in the distant sky, flying parallel to our car.

From that moment on I did not need any more proof that God existed. It had answered my challenge to prove to me that It was real, down to the very last word. But God was not through with me yet! There was more to come.

We arrived in California, picked up my wife's sister and her newborn son. Before leaving, we took the baby to its doctor for one final checkup. The doctor said he was in excellent health and would make the long journey to his new home in Pennsylvania without any problems.

By the time we reached the California-Arizona border, the baby was beginning to cry for hours at a time. As we traveled, his condition worsened, until he was crying around the clock and was unable to keep down any of his specially prepared milk formula. We decided to try and find a doctor.

The town of Cuba, Missouri, was only about five miles away. With half a tank of gasoline in the car, we decided to fill up in Cuba and drive on to St. Louis, where we thought we would stand a better chance of finding a good doctor. It would have taken us another four to six hours of driving, but we felt it was worth the effort. We filled up in Cuba and left. The car went dead just one mile outside of town. Every effort to start it failed. After about two hours we decided to walk back to Cuba, get a hotel room, and call a doctor from there.

We contacted a doctor at 1:30 a.m. He met us at his office, just a few blocks from the hotel. After examining the baby, he said we were awfully lucky we didn't drive on to St. Louis. The baby had developed an allergic reaction to his milk formula, which was putting poisons into his system, and had we driven on, the baby would have died. They rushed the baby to the hospital and pumped the toxins out of his stomach. Through the grace of God and Its loving intervention, the baby was saved from certain death. These events were beyond coincidence. They were truly a miracle.

But the real miracle was yet to come. I had the car towed to a local garage for repair. I left the car and returned several hours later to see what was wrong.

As I walked in, the mechanic had a strange look on his face. I asked him what he had found. He said that he couldn't find anything wrong with the car. I knew by the look on his face that there was more to come, so I asked him what he meant. He said, "Well, unless your car is different from every other car, the only thing I could find wrong was that you had a half tank of gasoline and a half tank of water."

Electrifying shivers ran through every fiber of my body. I went back to the gas station where we filled up our car. They checked their underground storage tanks. There was no sign of water, and no car either before or after us had experienced this problem.

How magnificent and loving God is! How very alive and real God is! How gentle and caring God is to take the time to communicate and express Itself in the life of someone of such little faith as me! I was humbled, and I was brought to my knees. And God, in Its merciful wisdom, answered my blatant and sacrilegious challenge to the word without harming one hair on the head of anyone I loved! From this moment on, I knew that I had to stop resisting Its calling and accept whatever work that It had for me to do, without any more doubts or indecision.

Who Are You?

I would ask, "How does it feel when I suggest to you that *you are* God? When I propose this question to my audience, I get a few nods of approval and sometimes a raised eyebrow or two. I'm quick to remind them that this is not going to become a religious discussion. We are here to talk about health and the healing process, and it has occurred to me that if we are to understand the healing process, we must first understand who we are and what our responsibility is to that process.

Imagine, if you will, that the oceans of the Earth represent the sum total of the Creator. Out of that giant ocean you take but a single drop of water and place it in the palm of your hand. Then you get out your microscope and you examine that single drop very carefully. In that drop of water you find all elements in exactly the same proportions as the ocean.

The Creator is the sum total of its creation.

Could there be a Creator without a creation? Could there be a creation without a Creator? The very term implies that one cannot exist without the other.

Science tells us that we have approximately 100 trillion cells in this beautiful body of ours. Imagine that I take a single cell from my body and place it on a plate and then leave. Later, a rather odd NASA scientist comes along, finds the plate, and says, "What have we here?" He gets out his microscope, examines the plate carefully, discovers that single cell, and exclaims, "Hi, who are you?"

That cell could give only one answer: "I am Rich."

Now the scientist places the cell in a lead box, puts the box in a spaceship and blasts it into outer space. One day a marooned astronaut discovers the spaceship, opens the box, gets out her microscope and says, "Well, hi, who are you?"

Again, it can give only one answer: "I am Rich. He is my Creator and I am his creation. I cannot deny my Creator nor can my Creator deny me, any more than you can deny *your* Creator or your Creator deny *you*."

Every time you step on a nail 100 trillion cells go, "Ouch!" Every time you laugh, 100 trillion cells laugh with you. Every time you step on a nail the Creator goes, "Ouch!" and every time you laugh the Creator laughs with you. The Creator is the sum total of Its creation. *It lives through Its creation.*

No, I did not say you were the Creator. I said you were God. No, I am not God over you, nor are you God over me. You are God only over your own creation and your own reality. It is *your* universe.

I cannot heal you, nor can you heal me. You can only heal yourself.

The Creator gave us free-will choice. If you are not satisfied with your creation, you can change it. The Creator will not *fix* it for you, nor will Jesus. When you ask for their help, they will assist you in every loving way possible. But true healing comes from within. *You are the ultimate healer.* Doctors have never healed a patient. Not even Jesus claimed to have healed anyone. The Master simply said, "It is by your faith that ye are healed." Jesus, physicians, those working with others, can only offer the tools by which individuals can heal themselves.

We are co-Creators with the Creator. The Creator made us in Its image and likeness, saying, "Go and create. I desire to experience all that I Am. Show Me what I am capable of creating. I want to experience My emotions. How can I experience love if I have never experienced fear. How can I experience joy if I have never felt sadness? I desire to experience all that I Am."

✦   ✦   ✦   ✦   ✦

A lamb is born and grows to maturity. A co-Creator shears the sheep. Another co-Creator takes the wool, washes and cleans it. It is then given to another co-Creator, who spins it into yarn, and to yet another who says, "I believe l will dye this yarn into many beautiful colors." Still another co-Creator says, "I will take this beautiful colored yarn and knit it into a magnificent sweater." Little did the lamb know what an important role it would play for its Creator.

Everything that you can see and perceive *is* God.

Think of all the cocreation that takes place around you every moment. Recognize the cocreation that you are involved in every day. Be aware of the drama that you have created in your life so that you may experience, learn and grow. Be aware of how your drama has helped others grow.

Would You Recognize God If He/She Knocked at Your Door?

A gentleman is sitting in his rocking chair on the front porch of his house in the path of rising floodwaters. A pickup truck drives by and stops. The driver leans out the window of his truck and says, "Mister, can I give you a ride?"

"Forget it," the man on the porch replies, "I'm working it out with God."

The waters continue to rise, and now the man is sitting on top of the porch roof. A boat comes along and the boatman, seeing the man's dilemma, speaks up. "Hey, mister, can I give you a lift?"

Once again he replies, "Forget it, I'm working it out with God."

Still later, as the floodwaters take their toll, the man is sitting on the rooftop of his house. A helicopter flies by. Seeing the situation, the pilot hovers overhead while a crewman shouts, "Hey, buddy, we'll throw you down a rope. Grab it and we'll pull you up."

Shouting at the top of his voice, he says, "Forget it, I'm working it out with God."

Finally, standing on his roof, up to his chin in water, he looks questioningly toward heaven. "God," he asked, "why haven't you heard me?"

Instantly a booming voice responds, "I sent you a pickup truck, a boat and a helicopter. What are you waiting for?"

The Creator works through its creation.

✧ ✧ ✧ ✧ ✧

A three-year-old child begged his parents to be left alone with his new infant sibling. Finally the parents agreed. Standing outside the door, they listened intently as they heard their three-year-old anxiously pleading, "Tell me about God. I'm forgetting."

If we are to understand the healing process,
we must first understand who we are
and what our responsibility is to the healing process.

The Vehicle

The vehicle was traveling down the street at an accelerated speed. Suddenly the traffic light ahead turned red. The vehicle applied its brakes and came to a stop at the intersection. For one minute the vehicle obediently remained in place, the engine idling, waiting, watching as vehicles from other directions took their turn crossing the street.

As the traffic light turned green and the intersection cleared, the vehicle revved its engine, slipped silently into gear and eased forward once again. When the road curved to the right, the vehicle also turned right, and when the road bore left, the vehicle responded in kind.

Upon arriving home, the vehicle pulled into the garage and rested comfortably in its familiar surroundings, awaiting the next outing. Sitting, cooling its engine, it thought, I am unable to do anything. I am only a vehicle. I cannot shift my gears or press my accelerator. Why, I can't even turn my steering wheel or apply my brakes. I am only a vehicle. I cannot do anything until someone sits behind the wheel, makes a conscious decision and takes command of my movements.

So often we are told that we are the sum total of our body, mind and soul. What does that really mean? In our society we spend a great amount of time focusing only on the vehicle. When we awaken, the vehicle arises, brushes its teeth, takes a shower, eats breakfast and prepares for its daily activities. When the light turns red, it stops and waits patiently for it to turn green. When it is ill, it travels to the doctor's office, sits obediently in the waiting room, occasionally smiling at the other vehicles sitting across the room. Occasionally the vehicle goes to the store to buy some fuel and to shop for a new covering. After all, why not? There is a big sale going on.

It is easy to become focused on the illusion (vehicle/body) and forget that the vehicle is unable to do anything until a conscious decision is made to give it direction.

Mind: The mass consciousness of the universe

in which all knowledge exists.

Thought: The energy of the mind put into motion.

Thought is the energy of the mind. Once thought enters the computer system (brain), it sets into motion a series of interactions that propel the vehicle into action. Each movement the vehicle makes is preceded by a thought. How long the vehicle serves us is totally dependent on the mind. The time may come when the vehicle is ready to be retired. Yet the eternal part of our Being lives on.

What Is Your Spiritual Journey?

Hanna Kroeger is considered by many to be one of the world's leading herbalists. She has assisted many in recovering their health. Ann Marie and I had the occasion to spend a few days at her center, known as The Chapel of Light. Shortly after arriving, we were engaged in a conversation with Hanna when she paused, looked at me and said, "Rich, would you like to be the guest speaker at my Sunday services?"

I replied, "Hanna, it would be my honor to do so."

The chapel was well-attended. Many had come a long distance to hear her bits of wisdom.

Services began with a brief address by Hanna, followed by a moving musical number played by her son, the organist. Immediately following the musical interlude, Hanna announced that this would be the only music we would hear at the services. She explained that the sewer had plugged up and that her son had to leave to take care of the problem. With that, her son left the chapel.

Hanna then announced me as her guest speaker. I looked at the congregation and paused momentarily in thought. With a pleasant smile I directed my question specifically to a member of the congregation. "On a spiritual scale of one to ten, with ten being the highest spiritual rating, how would you rate brushing your teeth in the morning?"

Giving it some thought, the person replied, "About a three."

Turning my gaze to another, I asked, "Using the same scale, how would you rate eating breakfast?"

"An eight," she replied without hesitation. "I consider nourishing my body important."

"And what about scrubbing the floor?" I inquired.

"Maybe a two" was the answer.

To the person in front of her I asked, "How would you rate going to Sunday services?"

His eyes sparkled. "That would have to be a ten," he responded.

As I looked around the chapel, I could see some knowing smiles of those who already were aware of the answer. "*Each* of those things that I have mentioned are a ten. You are a spiritual being experiencing a spiritual journey. Everything that you do, every breath that you take, is a spiritual experience." Smiling, I continued, "The reason that I bring this up at this time is because I find it comforting to know that our organist has gone to do his spiritual work."

As the laughter subsided, I said, "Often we have heard people say, 'I know I am here for a reason, but I haven't yet figured out what that is supposed to be.'"

Those people are correct; we are all here for a reason. There are no mistakes in the universe. I don't believe the Creator is sitting there saying, "Boy, I really messed up on this one. I had better call in the FDA, the FBI and the IRS to get this straightened out."

Everything is in divine perfection at all times. Everyone is exactly where they are supposed to be in the moment. As a soul, we have incarnated in physical form to experience and grow. Your spiritual journey in physical form began at the moment of conception. You have shared every thought, every emotion, every anxiety and the vibrational experience of every energy that your mother exposed herself to.

Some refer to the Earth as the "Earth school." Through our life experiences we learn, experience, and more importantly, we grow. It is important that we do not become so focused on the *lesson* that we fail to see the *value* we received from that lesson. The following story explains it quite well.

✧   ✧   ✧   ✧   ✧

Traveling down the pathway of our spiritual journey, many notice that the path is a series of stepping stones, each one representing a lesson. As they move to the next stone, they reach behind and pick up the one they have just left. Repeating this with each step,

they soon find they are so weighted with old lessons that they can no •
longer take another step forward in their journey.

The old lessons are no longer of value. Take the *value* that you
have received from these life experiences, which have allowed you to
grow in mind, body and spirit, and let the rest go. It is baggage that
no longer serves you.

Story Time

One Second of Time

I stood before a group, making a presentation. As the lecture progressed, the tennis ball that I held in my hand was beginning to create some questions in their minds. At one point I turned to a person in the audience and asked, "Have you ever played ball?"

"Yes," he responded.

Without hesitation, I threw the ball toward him and at the same time instructed, "Catch the ball!" His hand reached into the air and retrieved the ball. I turned to the audience and said, "You have just witnessed one of the most incredible things you will ever see." They looked again toward the person to whom I had thrown the ball, straining to see what they might have missed.

"In that one second," I stated, "I threw the ball in the air in the direction of this man and issued a command, 'Catch the ball!' The vibrations of the words that I had spoken traveled at an incredible speed and were picked up by his ears. These vibrations were relayed to his brain, which interpreted their meaning. Command signals were sent to every part of his body, instructing the appropriate cells to make chemical changes that would create muscle responses. His eyes measured the trajectory of the ball and calculated its exact time of arrival. The brain relayed this information to the body, and at the exact moment, 100 trillion cells responded in perfect harmony as his arm reached forward and his fingers opened and closed on the ball.

"During this entire time, the heart never missed a beat, the hair cells continued to multiply, his digestive system continued to function and the blood continued to race through his arteries and veins. Blood protein and lymph carrying life-giving nutrients flowed through the blood capillaries to nourish every cell of his body. The lymph system removed the waste products of the cells, while the liver and kidneys served their function to eliminate waste from the body. In this one second, six trillion chemical changes took place in his body and ten million cells replaced themselves and died.

"What an incredible world we have within each of us! We inhabit a world that replaces itself approximately every eleven months (except for the tiny hairlike neurons that send electrical impulses throughout the body) — bones are replaced every 90 days; a new liver every 45 days; new skin every 30 days; the lining of the stomach every 5 days. Even the DNA, which contains enough information to fill 4000 volumes the size of the Bible, changes every two months at the atomic level. We witness miracles every moment of the day, and we are rarely aware of their magnitude. And this miracle began with, 'Catch the ball!'"

Miracles are our everyday occurrences . . .

✧ ✧ ✧ ✧ ✧

The World Within

As a junior reporter for the *Daily City News*, I was surprised when the editor approached me and asked if I would write a cover story for the Sunday edition. I was excited. Imagine, me writing a feature story! I knew exactly what I was going to write about. I had been planning for this opportunity for a long time, and now it was here. I wanted to write a story that no one had ever done before. I was going to interview a single cell of the human body.

In order to do this, I must shrink into a microscopic body so that I can enter the human body. It wasn't as difficult as I thought it would be.

I suddenly found myself in a maze of incredible life forms that I had never seen before. The colors were breathtaking and ever changing. I realized that I had entered a universe that others were totally unaware of. I could feel the excitement growing within me.

But now I had to find a cell that I could interview. This might be more difficult than I first thought. This street seemed to be a major thoroughfare. I thought that if I walked down this way, I'd be able to find someone.

I had not walked a hundred feet before I saw someone walking toward me. He was wearing a white hat that matched his white suit. He appeared to be in a hurry.

"Pardon me, sir. I know you are busy, but would you have a few minutes? You see, I am a reporter for the *Daily City News* and I have been given an assignment to write a feature story. Would you have a moment to talk to me?"

He nervously looked at his watch, and then at me. "You're right, I *am* very busy," he replied, "but since you have apparently come a long distance, I'll give you a few minutes. Make it quick."

"Oh, thank you. I will get right to the point." My heart was pounding. I felt as though I was onstage with opening night jitters. Not quite sure where to begin, I nervously asked, "Who are you?"

He snapped back, "I'm a white cell. Can't you tell? All you have to do is look at my white hat. It's a dead giveaway."

"You're right, I should have known. Do you have a name?" I asked.

"Just call me Lucky. Everyone else does."

"Lucky," I asked, "tell me, what is it that you do?"

"I'm one of the good guys," he said. "You can always tell the good guys. We wear the white hats."

"Yes, Lucky," I repeated, "but what is it that you *do*?"

"As I said, I'm one of the good guys. It's my job to take care of the bad guys, and this world is loaded with them."

"Bad guys?" This was starting to get interesting. "What bad guys?" I asked.

"*You* know," Lucky said, "the guys in the black hats. They have different names. Some are called viruses and some are called bacteria. They come in all shapes, sizes and colors. If it wasn't for the black hats, it would be hard to tell them from the the regular folks out there. Sometimes it's all I can do to keep them under control."

"Wow! It really *does* sound like you're busy. Is it dangerous?"

"Dangerous?" he shouted. "Are you kidding? Hey, this is a high-risk job. It's kill or get killed out there. We don't mess around. I take my job very seriously."

"Lucky, you said 'we' don't mess around. You mean there are others besides you doing your work? Is that right?" I asked.

"You got it!" he snapped back. "There are millions of us trying to keep the world safe."

Millions, I thought. This was a bigger story than I had imagined. I could tell from the look on his face that Lucky was serious about his work. Finally I asked, "Then you work with a team of people in the work that you do?"

Lucky laughed. "Team? Are you kidding? It's every man for himself out there. I've got to look out for number one, and that's the guy I see in the mirror every morning when I wake up."

"Gosh," I replied, "I would have thought you'd work as a team." I noticed that Lucky was nervously looking at his watch, so I quickly went on. "I know you're busy, but there are just a few last questions I would like to ask before you go. Earlier you said that the people I call cells come in different sizes, shapes and colors. What colors are they?"

"You name it, we got it," he said. "White, black, yellow, red, brown and about any combination that you can imagine."

"Tell me," I asked, "what is the population of your world?"

"According to the last census, we have about 100 trillion."

"Whew! That's a lot of people," I said.

Lucky seemed amused at the look of amazement on my face. "You got *that* right."

"Quickly, tell me, Lucky, what are some of the major concerns in your world at this time?"

"Pollution," he replied without hesitation. "The water and air are polluted and getting worse. We're getting foods that are loaded with pesticides and chemicals. We are very concerned about all the toxic waste dumps that are building up all over the place. These are big problems. You know," he added, "if we don't find an answer to this soon, the whole world here is headed for a major collapse. Just look at the litter on the street that you just walked down. Sometimes I think people just don't care any more!"

The telephone beeper on Lucky's belt emitted a familiar beep tone. He checked it quickly and said, "I'm being called; I've got another emergency. I hope you got what you needed for your story." He turned and started off down the street.

I shouted after him, "Is there anything else I should know?"

"Yeah, the wars!" He turned to look at me.

"Wars?" I exclaimed. "*What* wars?"

"We've had wars as long as I can remember. Sometimes it's a civil war. Sometimes it's between different countries. There are times the kidney is at war with the liver. Other times the pancreas is at odds with the stomach. I could go on and on. If we could only negotiate peace, then everyone would live in unity and harmony instead of separation and disharmony. What a wonderful world this would be." He turned the corner and was gone.

I thought to myself, I've got the makings of a great story. I turned and started walking back up the way I had come, noticing the litter as I went.

The World Without

You wake up this morning and you are filled with excitement. All of your life you have wanted to travel into outer space, and you have been selected as one of a very special few to make a space flight leaving this very day. You get out of bed and prepare yourself for the journey. Standing in front of the mirror, you admire yourself in the handsome space suit you have selected.

Arriving at the spacecraft, you are given last-minute instructions, made secure in a special seat and readied for takeoff. You feel the push of gravity as the craft blasts off and accelerates to incredible speeds. It is difficult to describe your feelings of joy and wonderment as you anticipate seeing for the first time a world that so few have traveled to before.

Later, as you are sitting comfortably in your seat, you casually turn your head to look through the porthole window. Your eyes are drawn to a round blue-and-white object in the distance. You get out your telescope and focus on the object and, much to your surprise, you realize it is Mother Earth. Her beauty is indescribable. Your hand slides down the telescope and turns the magnification to its highest setting. Once again you look, and the view takes your breath away. As your eyes scan the Earth, you become keenly aware of six billion people, trillions of animals, birds, fish, insects and other life forms. Trillions of trees, bushes, flowers, grasses and plants of all types. For the first time you are aware of the rocks, mountains and water as living, vibrating life forms. You gaze in awe as you begin to understand the interactions of all this living energy, working together in divine harmony as one incredible life form. It is then that you realize that *the Earth is but a single cell of the Creator.*

You lean back in your seat as your mind digests your new discovery. Something catches your attention and your eyes are drawn to the porthole on the other side of the spaceship. As you gaze outward, you become aware of millions — no, billions — of stars, planets and celestial bodies. As your eyes scan the horizon, you become aware that *each galaxy, each universe, is but a single cell of the Creator.*

The World Around Us

Shortly after my son David graduated with majors in wildlife biology and wildlife management, he found himself in southern Africa as a wildlife game ranger. The last three of his seven years in Africa would be devoted to elephant research.

Over the years I have produced a number of films, and so I found myself traveling to Africa to produce a film about African wildlife and my son's research work. One afternoon, after several weeks living in the bush, David said that he wanted to spend some time studying the vegetation in the area to see if the elephants were destroying the food chain or instead, creating conditions that would result in greater abundance. Since I already had enough film footage of his research work, I suggested that he go without me. I found a comfortable tree to sit against with my camera, hoping to get some shots of elephants, lions or other large game that might come my way. As was typical for this time of year, the sky was clear and the warm sun was soothing to my body.

An hour had passed without signs of any animals. A moment later I happened to glance to the ground on my left. I was surprised to see a column of ants within twelve inches of my body. Each one was carrying a grain of food, walking with great determination in single file. I thought to myself, Where have they come from? I let my eyes follow along the column of ants in the direction from which they had come until the horizon met my eyes. I could not see the end of the column. Wow! I thought. Where are they going?

Once again my eyes began to follow the column, but this time in the direction that they were headed. Again my eyes reached the horizon, but I could not see their destination. I thought, In terms of human distance, this has to represent a hundred miles or more. It was then that I realized there was a second column of ants headed in the opposite direction, returning to the source for more food. I sat and watched, amazed at the dedication and organization of these industrious creatures. Then it struck me that I had been sitting here for the past hour totally unaware of this world existing a mere twelve inches away. A world so small I was completely unaware of it. And sitting next to them was a world too large for them to see.

Worlds within worlds within worlds.

I have often wondered, If I had accidentally stepped on that column of ants, would they have said, "It was an act of God"?

The Power of Love

Our schnauzer, Fritz, was more than just a dog; he was family. He would have been offended if anyone thought of him as a dog. A constant companion, Fritz would sleep on the bed at night, making himself comfortable as he snuggled against our legs.

One morning I awakened to find that Fritz could not put any weight upon one of his hind legs. I helped him to his feet and he stood on three legs, looking at me sadly, his other leg pointing straight out behind him. I had never seen any dog stand in that manner. I carried him outside for his morning outing, and again Fritz stood with his leg up, looking helpless.

On my way to work I dropped Fritz off at the veterinarian to have him examined. Carrying him inside, I set him on the floor in front of the reception desk. Immediately he began running around the room on all fours. I thought, You little devil! It reminded me of the time I had taken my car to a garage for them to investigate a strange noise, but when I got there, it wouldn't make the noise. I asked the vet to keep Fritz and observe him for the day, and my wife would pick him up after she got off work. After I informed my wife of the situation, she phoned the vet's office and asked them to clean his teeth while he was there. After all, Fritz was ten years old and overdue for a teeth cleaning.

Later that day the vet phoned my wife to tell her that in order to clean teeth, they must sedate the animal and put a tube down its throat so it can breathe. However, they could not get the tube down Fritz's throat. Upon examination, they found a tumor on his tonsils about the size of a small cigar, which they removed.

"We suspect cancer," the vet said. "I have shown it to two of my colleagues and they agree. We are sending it to the laboratory for a biopsy and it will take about ten days to get a report. There is also a large amount of blood in the stool, so we would like to keep him another day to try to control the bleeding," he added.

After being informed of the situation, I calmly said to my wife and another couple who were present that Fritz would be healed. There was never any doubt in my mind.

After picking Fritz up from the vet's, I found that he was indeed passing blood in the stool. We had to pen him up at night and place papers on the floor.

Beginning that evening and every evening for four days, I worked with Reiki energy (the universal energies of love), allowing the energy of pure love to emanate from my hands as I placed them on his head, throat, chest and stomach. His body burned with a high temperature. I would place him on my stomach and chest while I lay in bed and I would fall asleep in that position, awakening later when he became restless.

On the the fifth day I prepared to leave for an important convention for my company. I was disappointed that I could not stay and continue working with Fritz. As I began shaving, Fritz raced through the bath and bedroom with the vitality of a two-year-old. I noticed that his hair was shiny and there was a sparkle in his eyes we had not seen for a long time.

The following evening I phoned my wife. She informed me that the vet had called to say the tumor was benign.

After the call I sat on the edge of the bed in my hotel room, deep in thought. Not having been through this experience before, I was puzzled. I was still confident about the intuitive answers I had received that confirmed the vet's earlier belief that the tumor was malignant. The more I thought about this, the more convinced I became that I was correct.

I realized that there are universal truths expressed as "as above, so below" or "what exists on one plane exists on all planes." For example, what exists in the physical plane also exists on the emotional, or etheric plane, and vice versa. I already knew that the vibrations of each person or animal are truly individual and that there are no two beings alike in the universe.

A good analogy is today's pager. We see thousands of persons carrying a little black box on their belt that will emit a beep tone, alerting them that they have received a phone call. Although there are thousands of little black boxes, only one will receive a signal when its unique phone number is dialed. That box is attuned to that specific frequency and no other.

When I wipe a dowsing rod with a silver quarter, I energize the rod for that frequency so I can locate that quarter. If I were to cut the quarter in half, I could find each half separately. Therefore, if I were to energize the rod to Fritz's frequency and then remove a part of his body (a tumor), I could also find that part.

Fritz's energy field (the sum total of all that he is, mind, body and spirit) has an individual frequency that is unique in the universe. When you transfer energy on one plane, it is transferred on all planes. It is a universal truth. Therefore, when the healing energy of love was transferred to Fritz, it was received on all planes of his existence.

In other words, as the healing of the vibrations of disease in Fritz's body took place, it also took place at all other levels of his being. As his body changed, so did his extracted tumor, regardless of its location in the universe. Healing energy, the same as thought, goes anyplace in the universe instantly. And like the telephone call, there is only one receiver.

Upon arriving home, my wife told me the rest of the vet's conversation. He had said, "Mrs. Work, when I removed the tumor, I would have bet anything it was malignant. It was the ugliest tumor I had ever seen, and all my staff agreed it was malignant. But the lab report said it was benign. I am very happy for you and your dog, but I don't understand how I could have been so wrong."

How often do doctors call it "spontaneous remission" or decide that they have made a misdiagnosis simply because they cannot otherwise explain a healing? True, there is a certain percentage of diagnostic errors under normal circumstances. But love heals. Prayer heals. And the scientific-minded may never understand.

Love is the unspoken Prayer
that resonates through all Time and Space and Beyond,
and in all languages.

The Human Energy Field

The aura (energy field) that surrounds our body projects energy outward like the light of an incandescent light bulb. For descriptive purposes it is usually shown as several layers, but in reality each energy is an integral part of every other part of our being. Our emotional body is not separate from our physical body, nor is our mental body separate from the emotional body. Each one is simply an aspect of the whole.

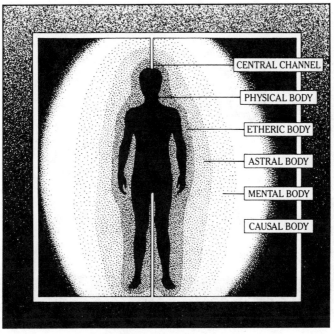

The Human Energy Field
From *Vibrational Medicine* by Dr. Richard Gerber.

Dr. Richard Gerber, writes, referring to this diagram: "We can see the energetic expression of the multidimensional human being.

Although perhaps not all of these higher subtle bodies are photographable, it is quite likely that the etheric and possibly the astral may be captured and measured with sophisticated imaging systems such as the EMR scanner or its forerunners."

The Holographic Principle

Science has demonstrated that you can take a holographic picture (a single apple was used in the demonstration), then cut off a small corner of the film and examine it under a laser light, a smaller, yet intact, whole apple can be seen. The hologram could be cut into one hundred separate pieces, yet each piece would contain the whole image of the apple.

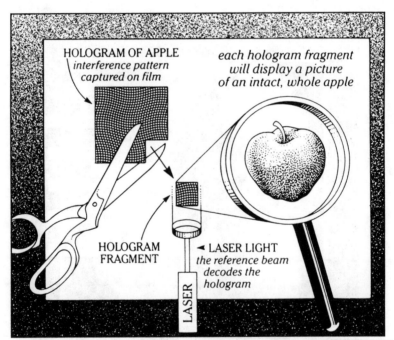

HOLOGRAM OF APPLE
*interference pattern
captured on film*

*each hologram fragment
will display a picture
of an intact, whole apple*

HOLOGRAM
FRAGMENT

◄ LASER LIGHT
*the reference beam
decodes the
hologram*

LASER

The Holographic Principle: Each Piece Contains the Whole
From *Vibrational Medicine* by Dr. Richard Gerber.

As Above, So Below
The Holographic Principle in Nature

How then does one apply holographic theory to understanding phenomena in nature? The simplest place is to begin with the human body.

Dr. Gerber writes: "At a highly symbolic level, the holographic principle that 'every piece contains the whole' can be seen in the cellular structure of all living bodies. Scientific discoveries in the world of cellular biology have demonstrated that every cell contains a copy of the master DNA blueprint, with enough information to make an entire new body from scratch."

That same cell is also capable of creating a new organ or any other part of the body. It only needs directions from a higher intelligence —you. What are your "orders of the day"? What are your thought patterns?

✧ ✧ ✧ ✧ ✧

Everything in the universe is electromagnetic energy, and all energy has a frequency. Energy is a *living form*. Objects that we do not consciously refer to as alive, such as rocks, metals, clouds, etc., are in reality living forms. Even the leaf that has fallen from the tree and turned brown is living energy. It has merely changed its form.

The Phantom Leaf Phenomenon

Dr. Gerber writes: "Studies by I. Dumitrescu in Rumania, utilizing a scanning technique based on electrographic process, added a new twist to the phantom leaf effect. Dumitrescu cut a circular hole in the leaf and then photographed the leaf with his electographic equipment. The image revealed was that of a tiny intact leaf with a smaller hole in it. The smaller leaf appeared inside the area where the circular portion of the leaf had been cut away."

Just as the hologram shows the "whole" within each segment, the leaf would also seem to confirm the holographic nature of the organizing energy field that surrounds all living systems. Is it not just possible that we are the holographic image and likeness of the Creator? We are the Whole within the Whole of the Creator.

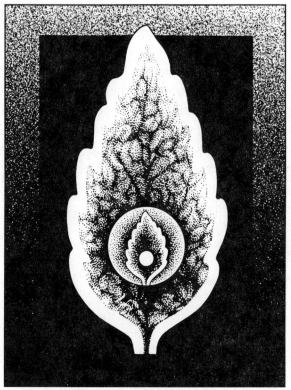

Phantom Leaf Phenomenon
From *Vibrational Medicine* by Dr. Richard Gerber.

Can there be a Creator without a creation?
Can there be a creation without a Creator?

Discovering the Healer Within

It was approaching one o'clock in the afternoon and the temperature had barely reached forty-one degrees as Don arrived at the small airport. The ground was still frozen, but this was to be expected during March in Illinois. It seemed a strange time to be doing another free-fall with the parachute team. For Don, this would be his fifty-second jump. After orientation, he hurriedly put on his chute and joined the others.

As the plane slowly rose to 10,000 feet, he reflected on what he was about to do. Familiar with the routine, he would free-fall at 120 miles per hour to 4000 feet, then open his chute and slow to 15 miles per hour, pick his spot and touch down for another successful jump.

It was time. Without hesitation, Don stepped through the open door into weightlessness, arms and legs spread wide in the typical free-fall position. It was exhilarating to be free, as if he were separated from the busy world that he had just left, and yet he was a part of the totality of the Earth and all of its wonders. Nothing to interrupt his thoughts other than the air rushing by.

He was conscious of the altitude. Six thousand, five thousand, four thousand feet. Pull the cord. The chute unfurled and he felt the familiar tug as the acceleration slowed.

Without warning, one of the other team members, still in free-fall and traveling at 120 miles per hour, ripped through his chute like a cannonball through a watermelon. He heard someone shout, "I'm sorry!"

Four of the seven sections of the chute were completely gone, and the other three flailed in the air like a trailing comet. The action that followed left Don completely snarled in the cords. Hanging upside down, his legs and arms wrapped not unlike a mummy, he fought to free his reserve chute. Finally, he wrenched it open, but it also became a part of the entanglement. The trailing sections had slowed his fall to about 65 miles per hour. Thoughts raced through his mind. "God, please let me live. If you let me live, I will never jump again." The ground was rushing toward him at an incredible speed. He could see that he would land in an open field about 100 yards square surrounded on all sides by woods. Five hundred feet. "God, don't let me feel any pain."

Head first, he hit the frozen ground and counted as he bounced three times. With his face buried in the dirt and unable to move, he lay there unaware if he were dead or alive. The person who ripped through his chute managed to follow him down and landed nearby. "Don," he questioned, "are you alive?"

Don, face in the dirt, struggled to reply, "Are you dead?"

"No," his companion answered, "we are both alive."

It was ninety minutes before the paramedics arrived. Don lay there unable to move. God had answered his prayer – there was no pain. Almost every major bone in his body had been broken. His face had been crushed, and one eye was hanging loosely from his face. The paramedics literally rolled him onto the stretcher; there were no solid parts to hold onto. He felt like he was playing a part in a Keystone Cops movie as the medics tripped and stumbled, dropping him several times as they tried to negotiate a path through the woods.

Arriving at a small local hospital, they gave him shots for pain, but they could do nothing more for him through the night. They did not expect him to live. The next day he was transferred to a larger hospital; again they waited for him to die. A day passed before a doctor asked, "Do you want me to do something?"

"Yes, for God's sake, do something," Don said, "but I want you to promise that you will allow anyone I ask for to visit me for as long as I want – those who will assist me in prayer and with healing energy work."

"You have my assurance," the doctor replied. With that, he began to do massive reconstruction surgery on his unrecognizable face with an eye that still dangled out of its socket.

Don had already started his healing work. "It began even as I lay in the field where I landed," he recalls. Those working with prayer, hands-on healing, Reiki energy, came freely and often, sometimes working around the clock. A passing parade of doctors came to look at his broken body. They agreed that if he were to live at all, he would be in the hospital for eight to twelve months, and would still probably be crippled.

Twenty-two days from the time he was admitted, he checked himself out of the hospital and went home. He continued his healing work, and four weeks later he stepped from his wheelchair. In six more weeks he would put his walker away for the last time.

Don had discovered the Healer Within.

Auric Photographs

Pam, two hours after the Healing.

Pam, before the Healing (p. 99).

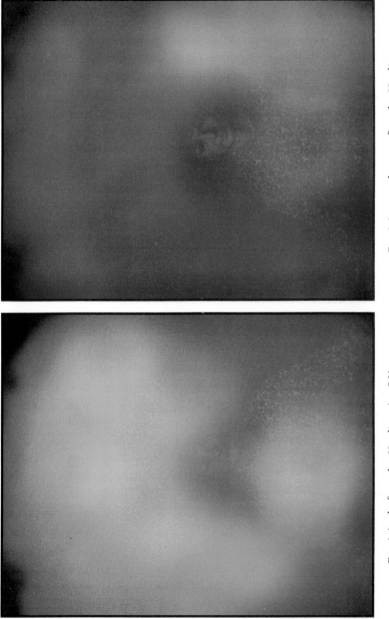

Patricia, two hours after the Healing.

Patricia, before the Healing (p. 99).

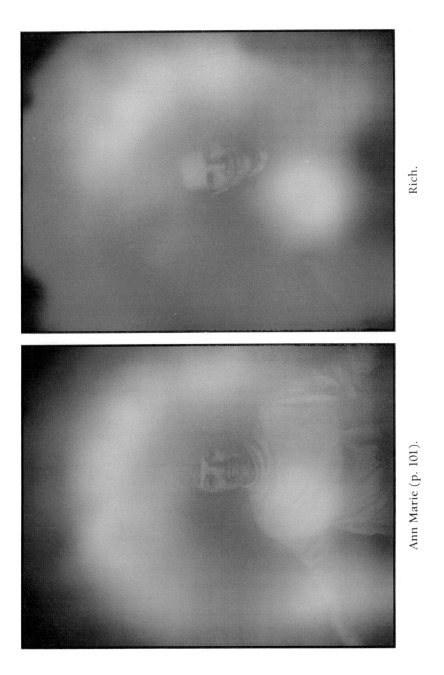

Rich.

Ann Marie (p. 101).

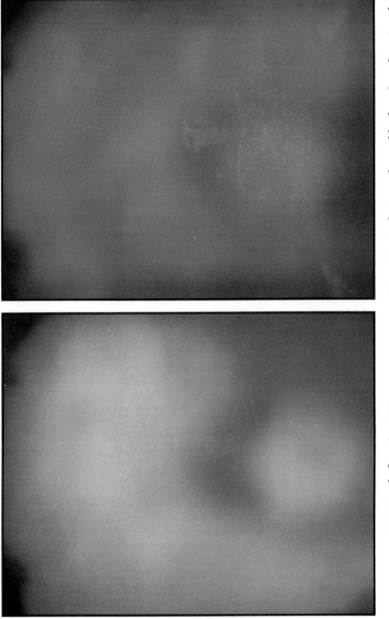

Five minutes later, embraced by her Guardian Angel.

Patricia, before (p. 257).

Healing Is the Process of Letting Go

We live in a society that has learned that if your car develops a problem, you take it to the garage – they'll fix it!

If the television loses its picture, take it to the electronics repair department – they'll fix it!

When the washing machine doesn't work, you call the appliance repairman – he'll fix it!

And when the body begins to malfunction, you take it to the body shop (hospital) – they'll fix it!

Fix it they will try – but *fix it* they will not.

I do not intend to discredit the medical community. They offer many tools that can assist in crisis care, and may allow the patient the opportunity to discover that true healing comes from within.

The human experience is not a machine made up of replaceable parts. It is a living consciousness manifested in physical form.

✧   ✧   ✧   ✧   ✧

Meditation is the process of letting go; of clearing the mind of all thoughts, all worries, all anxieties, the activities of your busy day, the cobwebs of the mind; of allowing yourself to go into your quiet space within your mind; and of allowing the inner being to be expressed.

To be psychic is the process of letting go; of clearing once again those thoughts and beliefs that have accumulated to clutter the mind; of going within your inner being and listening to the intuitive consciousness that has been there all along.

> **Psychic:** The connection between your perceived reality – your body; and your real reality – your soul.

Being spiritual is the process of letting go; letting go of old thought patterns and belief systems that have become your limitations; and allowing yourself to rediscover the Divine Creation that you have always been and always will be.

Healing is the process of letting go; letting go of old beliefs that have created limitations. Letting go of emotions, fears and judgments. Letting go of old laws and agreements that have interfered with your ability to move forward in life. Releasing bonds that have interfered with free-will choice. Healing is the process of letting go and recognizing the perfection of the Divine Creation within. Healing is not a process of trying, but one of allowing.

✧   ✧   ✧   ✧   ✧

Although this has been said before, it bears repeating. Let's make it absolutely clear who the true healer is. Each one of us is our own healer. Healing comes from within. No one else can do it for you.

There is no wrong way to assist someone with a healing when it is done in love, for it is love that has the healing energy. Healing does not have to be done by the numbers. There are as many ways to assist in the healing as there are those who desire to receive a healing.

To assist others in their healing is to offer it in love. It is not to interfere with the free-will choice of another. It is not trying to "fix" something you see as imperfect. It is *assisting* another — if and when they ask for your assistance, and not before. You cannot fix anyone who does not want to be fixed. Many have tried, but none have succeeded.

When someone requests your help, then and only then do you have permission to assist.

✧   ✧   ✧   ✧   ✧

One physician explains, "When a patient comes to me and says, 'Doctor, here I am, make me well!' I respond, 'There is nothing that I can do to help you. You would be better advised to take your money and take a nice vacation. It is money better spent.'

"However, if a patient says, 'Doctor, here I am, can you help me?' I then advise, 'Yes, I can be of assistance to you.' I know by their very words that they have made a commitment to become an active participant in the healing process. Then and only then can I assist my client."

✧ ✧ ✧ ✧ ✧

Learning how to ask permission: Too often I witness a situation in which a person who has a physical problem is approached by another who says, "Give me a minute, I can fix that." That person has not given permission. In fact, they may not even desire to be fixed. At least not just yet.

We live in a society that suggests we pray for those who are not well. I know of many well-intentioned people who belong to prayer groups and healing circles that offer prayers (healing energy) in an effort to see others become well. To do so without the permission of the person for which it is directed is to interfere. No, I am not going to suggest that you stop praying, but I would suggest that you consider offering it in the following manner.

I now call forth [name] to stand before me

as I stand before you – in Love.

On your behalf

I offer you this prayer to accept or reject

according to your Free-Will Choice.

[Add your prayer.]

Even if it is your intent to offer a healing to the Earth itself, I still suggest that you do so in the manner described above. Even the Earth is one of God's children and has a consciousness and free-will choice.

Violation of Free-Will Choice in any form is rape.

Not everyone desires to become healed.

I have never met anyone who would look you in the eye and tell you, "I don't want to get well." At the conscious level everyone will deny that they want their disease. But many people have worked hard to manifest their illness and they are not about to allow you to deny them the rewards of their efforts.

In a small gathering I met a lady whose opening comment was about the pain she was suffering. It dominated her conversation. She described it in great detail as her husband sat patiently listening nearby. When I would try to change the subject, she would quickly return the conversation to her problem. Her journey was one of going from doctor to doctor, but no one was able to help her. Her pain was so severe that her husband had to be home right after work. She was totally dependent on him.

He had to drive her everywhere, do the housework and do the cooking. Her needs limited him to going directly to work and returning home immediately after. It was clear that she had set the guidelines for his activities. To me, it was also clear that she had created the conditions that allowed her to set the rules. She was in absolute control of her mate.

There was no way anyone was going to deny her her pain.

❖   ❖   ❖   ❖   ❖

Another person had been lonely most of her life. She thought, "I have no friends; no one ever comes to visit with me." Then one day she was diagnosed with a terminal disease. Suddenly she was visited by an endless number of friends and acquaintances who brought their best wishes and sympathy. This was wonderful. Her life was being fulfilled according to her desires. She had placed her thoughts into universal consciousness, reinforced by desire, and the universe had manifested it well. To her friends, she always said that although she was diagnosed as terminal, she really did not want to die. But her subconscious understood that she did not really want to get well, either. What she truly desired was to maintain an equilibrium that would allow her to continue to receive attention from her new-found friends. She lived for many years, neither getting worse nor getting better. We truly do create our own realities.

Some find the world they live in too unfriendly, too chaotic, too fearful, too judgmental; and therefore through the subconsciousness they create a condition to manifest a disease and leave this world. "I no longer want to be here."

Many are not aware of the power of thought. Imagine a person who often comments, "Sometimes I wish I were dead." Later, after a disease manifests, that same person's reaction is, "There is no way you're going to convince me that I created this disease."

Affirmations — How and Why They Work

Every thought you think, every word you speak, is a prayer. It is a prayer that resonates throughout every vibration of your mind, body and soul. Any formulation of thoughts or words become a prayer. The words of those who choose witchcraft or satanic rites become their prayers.

Thoughts of fear will deplete your life-force energy. They are powerfully destructive.

Thoughts of love will heal, and are powerfully constructive.

An affirmation is a prayer that you affirm to yourself.

An invocation is a prayer that you invoke on another.

Since thought is the most powerful energy in the universe, then affirmations — designed to achieve a specific result by releasing energies that interfere with your free-will choice and your ability to move forward in your life according to your heart's desire — become powerful tools to assist in the healing process.

✧ ✧ ✧ ✧ ✧

Asbestos Poisoning

Although I had done a considerable amount of healing work on myself prior to this illness, it is the following affirmation that I personally focused on as my lungs healed. I am unaware of any modality in either orthodox or alternative medicine that is capable of doing what was done in my healing.

I had removed a tile floor from my basement with an electric hammer and chisel. I had breathed in clouds of dust as a result, not thinking to use a dust mask. My lungs were severely congested, and it was only after I had finished the job that I became aware that I had removed *asbestos* tile. The result was labored breathing and restricted lung capacity. As a child, I had been a severe asthmatic, and I knew what labored breathing was like.

Several years later I traveled to Dallas to work a convention for my company. Shortly after I arrived, I began to experience a high fever. Believing I had the flu, I instructed the rest of our group to set up the booth at the convention and told them I would have the flu under control in a day or so. I had been focusing on a very powerful affirmation at that time, and now I found myself repeating it again and again for my fever.

From the Divine Love that flows through my Being:

I open my Mind, Body and Soul,

and ask that you fill my Being

with your infinite Love,

your infinite Healing,

your infinite Protection,

your infinite Power and Wisdom.

I now call forth my Grand Adventure,

in feelings and emotions,

in all things that come in Light and Love

that will bring me Happiness and Joy.

So be it!

For five days I remained confined to my hotel room with a high temperature. My body felt like it was in an oven. I would cough up large amounts of phlegm. All my meals were sent to my room, but I was unable to eat much of anything. I could do little more than lie in bed. Three times I passed out, collapsing on the floor, unaware of how long I had been unconscious. Finally I called the front desk and suggested that I could use some help. They called a taxi and sent me to the hospital.

I arrived at the intensive care unit, and since I had a history of heart disease, their tests focused on my heart. I told them it was not my heart, but that had little impact. They gave me intravenous fluids with electrolytes, stating that I was dehydrated from the fever. I agreed with them and asked why they didn't simply give me some Gatorade to drink – it would be less expensive. Four hours and several thousand dollars later, I called a taxi and returned to my hotel.

My fever broke, and shortly after, I was able to return to work. Throughout this entire time I had repeated the affirmation over and over. I did not realize until sometime later that I had just partici-pated in a Healing. I had desired a healing. I had called it forth. Yet, caught in the drama of the healing itself, I was totally unaware that my body was purging itself of the asbestos in my lungs. Every-thing that I had experienced was the healing taking place. The fever was the body's way to eliminate what was no longer desirable. I had created my own healing. We always do.

Samuel

Samuel came to me at the urging of a friend. He had no idea who I was or what work I did. He only knew that he trusted his friend and that he was looking for his own personal miracle.

During the previous thirteen years, Samuel had been diagnosed with a disease known as Crohn's (deterioration of the colon), later to be called irritable bowel syndrome/colitis. No matter what it was called or what was prescribed, it did not change the symptoms or return him to the quality of life he so deeply desired. For the past eight years he had daily experienced abdominal pains, bleeding from both the bladder and the bowel, and loss of bowel control. His journey had taken him in and out of hospitals, where they gave him every test known for the disease. No matter what was tried, nothing changed.

The following are Samuel's comments:

"The answers to the path that I was walking have always led me to search within, and I felt that the disease was subject to something within my reach. However, I needed a teacher to take me over the top. Rich and Ann Marie have been those teachers. After a two-hour appointment with Rich and following Ann Marie's advice to raise my level of wellness, the bleeding in the urine and bowels stopped within twelve hours. I regained control within one month and had a doctor's examination to confirm that all signs of the disease were in remission, with no sign of disease ever having been present. I continue to use their teachings for continued growth and healing."

Susan

I had been invited to a Saturday dinner with a couple I had known for several years. As the meal was completed, Susan suddenly turned to me and exclaimed, "Rich, see this growth on the side of my nose? I just came from the doctor today and they have diagnosed it as malignant. The doctor informed me that a radical operation would be needed."

Susan was very familiar with the work I do. She had gone through a healing several months before and knew the power of affirmations. I smiled and asked, "Susan, what is it that *you* desire?"

Almost before I could finish my question, she responded, "I want it gone."

"May I assist you in bringing this about?" I asked.

"Of course," she replied.

I asked her to stand up and place a finger on the growth on her nose, then asked her to repeat the following affirmation:

From the Divine Love that flows through my Being

and in the name of the Creator God,

I command that this growth and all conditions

relating to it be gone.

I gave her a friendly hug and said, "Rest well."

Eight o'clock the next Monday morning, I sat in her husband's office, drinking a cup of tea and discussing the business at hand. He stopped abruptly in the middle of a sentence, looked at me excitedly and said, "Rich, I almost forgot to tell you. Susan's growth fell off yesterday, thirty-six hours after you were at the house."

You can release a disease as quickly as you can manifest it.

You can remanifest a disease as quickly as you can release it.

Marlin

Marlin said his doctor had confirmed that the two growths on his shoulder were malignant and had recommended that they be surgically removed as soon as possible. I asked Marlin, "What is it that you desire?" "I would like them gone," he replied. I asked if he would consider saying some affirmations. He agreed. Sitting across the room from him, I led him through the affirmations as they are outlined in this book. A few weeks later his doctor confirmed that the two growths had totally disappeared.

Dan

"My work is hard and physical, and when I injured my back the pain was excruciating. Doctors would not permit me to work. Several months passed, and still there was no improvement regardless of what medical care, traction or medication they offered. A friend asked me if I was enjoying my pain. I replied no. She asked if I wanted to be released from my pain, and I said, 'Of course.' She said that she had two friends she felt could help, and that all they needed was my permission. My pain was severe, so I did not hesitate to say, 'Yes, they have my permission.'

"That night, unknown to me, Rich and Ann Marie did what is known as long-distance healing. I knew nothing about this or what they would be doing. I knew only that I had given my permission to accept my healing. The next morning, to my surprise, I awoke pain-free. It was as though I had gotten a new life. No pain. No sign of ever having had a back problem, and it remains so many months later."

Sonia

Sonia sat before me with a troubled expression on her face. The beautiful young woman, in the prime of her life, commented that she had just come from a specialist who had told her that she would never be able to become pregnant and have a child.

"I had two tubular pregnancies and a miscarriage," she explained. "The operations that followed removed one fallopian tube and the other was severed. After months of repeated trips to a doctor, he agreed that he would try to repair the one tube. That was more than nine months ago, so I decided to make an appointment with you."

The expression on her face told me there was nothing more important to her at this time.

After listening to her concerns, I asked, "Sonia, what is it that *you* desire?"

"I want to have a child," she said with great emotion.

Three weeks later, at her first ovulation, she became pregnant. Nine months later she gave birth to a beautiful, healthy, seven-pound, twelve-ounce baby girl.

Sonia wrote: "It all seems very coincidental, but my session with Rich gave me the strength and assurance that anything in life is possible. Whether it is due to the medical profession or Rich, I must thank Rich for making me a believer."

Charlotte

"A tragic car accident left my husband dead and myself severely injured. More than twenty years later, after multiple operations, I was still in severe pain resulting from whiplash to the upper verte-brae. Sacroiliac joints were compressed; I had hearing loss, scar tissue in my left shoulder, a break in my left humerus at the point of deltoid attachment; nerve damage in my left hand that had left three fingers that would not function properly. There was much scar tissue in my abdomen; both hips were dislocated (much pain); I had no feeling in much of toes and feet. I also had dislocated knees, weak legs that give out at times, bladder problems, sinus headaches, not to mention the severe pain I experienced most of the time. I was also dealing with fused vertebrae in my lower back, torn cartilage in my left ankle, chronic fatigue, mercury poisoning, lungs burned by bug spray, and three tumors on the left thyroid.

"At the end of my appointment with Rich, during which I could feel the warmth of the love of God flow through every part of my being, he asked me to stand up and lovingly try out my new body. I got up cautiously and moved, stretched, bent over, raised each leg one at a time onto the massage table, and to my surprise found that there was no pain — none. My fingers worked perfectly and feeling returned in areas where there was none before. My back and all joints were limber, and a few days later the tumors were gone. I had volunteered to allow Rich to conduct my healing before an interested group of therapists. As I looked around, tears of joy caressed their faces."

✧ ✧ ✧ ✧ ✧

As I witness each healing, I stand in awe of the healing powers of the human experience, knowing that I have healed no one save myself. It has only been my honor to have assisted and witnessed their healing.

Not everyone chooses to give a testimonial on their healing. Most simply want to get over this hurdle and go on with their life without becoming a public attraction. Some may share their story, and a few will even deny their healing. The following is such a case.

Carl

A gentleman came to me having been diagnosed with a terminal disease, and said he had been told that he had less than a year to live. As a successful businessman, he was seeing his dream falling apart before his eyes, as well as what would happen to his lovely wife and children. He had little knowledge of the type of work I do. He was simply looking for his miracle. I asked what he desired to change in his life. When he replied, "I have been away from my God too long," I knew that he had made a commitment to make a change within his Being. We completed the two-hour session.

A month later I received a phone call from him in which he said, "Rich, I just want to keep you up to date with what is going on with me. I have had two more diagnoses from separate specialists since I met you, and they both confirm that I have no disease in my body, and I am really upset with that first doctorwho misdiagnosed me."

Such a statement is understandable when you consider that he had already told all his family and friends that he was going to die. He had a choice of trying to explain why he went to someone like me or simply denying that he ever had a problem. I urge everyone to obtain a second opinion in such matters, but I also reminded him that he had been handed a laboratory report that confirmed his condition, and that he might want to reconsider that he did in fact receive the healing he had asked for and had been given a second chance to review the direction he was taking in his life.

❖ ❖ ❖ ❖ ❖

There is an old saying, "You can't see the forest for the trees. All you can see is that damn tree in front of you." However, if you were in a hot-air balloon high above the forest, you could see yourself, the tree in front of you, the entire forest and the pathway leading into and out of the forest. It is always good advice to remove yourself from the drama and look at your journey from a higher perspective. What was the *value* of the lesson you have experienced? What was its message?

Healings Come in Many Forms

People were busily engaged in playing the popular game of "What's in it for me?" Many had built homes, put up fences, bought the extra car and a boat, taken on extra jobs to ensure that they could meet the payments those luxuries imposed. So busy were the lives of many that they had not taken time to get to know their neighbors. Then one day, in a matter of minutes, a devastating hurricane unleashed its fury through a wide section of the state.

Houses and trees were leveled for miles in all directions. As far as the eye could see, it looked as if the Creator had played a gigantic game of pick-up-sticks.

Standing among the rubble of their homes with only the shirts on their backs, the people looked around at their neighbors and said, "Everything we have worked for all our lives is gone." In that moment a healing took place. In that moment, all of them had to reevaluate their priorities. They were alive, and for the most part still in good health. They had their families. No one was any better or worse off than his neighbor. So, rolling up their sleeves, they all pitched in together to rediscover those new priorities and make new acquaintances with the people next door.

The same thing takes place whether it is a flood or an earthquake. I do not intend to make light of the losses of others. Twice I have been through a fire and lost everything. My point is simply this: If you have anything that you cannot live without, it has become your master. It now owns you. There is nothing wrong in having possessions unless those possessions possess you. We are only the caretaker of these wonderful creations for the time that we have them. Enjoy them.

Kirlian Photography

For many years Kirlian photography has been used to record the energy fields surrounding the physical body in both black and white and in color. Photos before and after their healing have given validation to both Pam and Patricia of the change that had taken place (see pages 83 and 84.) The colors seen in the photos taken before their healing would indicate a great amount of emotional and physical stress. Both were experiencing pain. Photos taken following their appointment reflect the powerful healing energies. Photos were also taken twenty-four hours later (not shown) to verify that the healing energies were still present, and that their auric fields had not regressed back to their former state.

Interpreting Auric Colors

There are many interpretations of the colors in the auric field. This is understandable, as it is reported that the aura may have as many as 1000 or more layers, each layer relating to a different aspect of one's Being. I have consulted with a professional therapist who works with auras and can actually see them. The following are her comments:

There are many factors to be considered when interpreting the aura; therefore, although the photos show several specific points, the descriptions listed below are general in nature and not intended as a diagnostic tool.

The auric photos will show several specific points.

The Heart Center: Varies from mild to intense energy and may reflect a different color than other parts of the aura.

Reminder: References to "left" (or "right") refer to the colors on the subject's left (while sitting for the photo) and not those on the photo as you face it.

—Left Side (Future): The color on your left side is normally the vibration coming into your being. The closer it is to you, the sooner it will be felt —in a few moments, a few hours, or as long as a few months.

—Center (Experience): The color seen over your head is what you experience for yourself now. It is the color that would best describe you. If the color is high, it could mean aspirations, or what you wish to be.

—Right Side (Expression): The color on your right side is traditionally the energy being expressed, the vibrational frequency most likely seen or felt by others around you. Many times your friends will think that this is the energy of which you are made. However, it is what you are putting out to the world.

One Therapist's Color Interpretation

The aura is not necessarily seeing single distinct colors, but rather a combination of shades. Different combinations would be interpreted differently.

Red: Emotion, anger, inflammation, physical problems in an active state.

Orange: Reflects the emotional more than the physical and may reflect sexual arousal. Orange by itself is not considered a problem color, but when intermixed with yellow it becomes problematic. Intense red-orange is intense passion, not to be confused with pure red, which is problematic.

Yellow: Yellow is not a healthy color. It is the first stage of problematic colors. There are many shades of yellow — the lighter shades are less problematic; the more intense the shade, the more problematic. Yellow can indicate stress and a depletion of your energy. It can also reflect fear and emotional or physical stress.

Violet: A very high spiritual, healing energy.

Green: Emerald green is an intense healing color. However, when intermixed with yellow it indicates that problems still exist. This combination should not be seen as a problem, but as a problem being resolved by the healing energies of green.

Blue: Blue is a very healthy color. The lighter the blue and the more white light that has entered, the greater the movement toward the higher spiritual energies. A darker blue may be interpreted as defensive, less open, self-protective, but not negative. Blue of any shade is a positive color.

White: Indicates purity. High levels of spiritual vibrations.

Gold: Not normally seen in this type of photography, but interpreted as someone special — that they are about to do, are doing, or have done something special of a higher vibration. I mention the color here because I note that some soft pastel yellows may also be seen as a shade of gold. Gold is considered on the same high level as white.

Bright White or Blue Balls of Light: Either of these appearing over and to the left side of the person reflects the clear higher vibrations and indicates the absence of distorted energy patterns.

Translucent Aura: Many auras are so dense that you can barely see the person within the aura. Others — for example, Ann Marie and Rich — have translucent auras (see page 85). I usually see this only in those who have been taking the *Harmonic Essences,* and who are on a higher vibrational level. I can tell how long a person has been on the Harmonic Essences by the translucence of the aura.

✧   ✧   ✧   ✧   ✧

The terms "light" and "love" are synonymous. The pure vibrations of love resonate in the full color spectrum, just like light as it passes through a prism. People who see auras see the *light,* pure colors of love and the *dark,* distorted frequencies of fear. As people's consciousness rises and the distorted frequencies of fear are eliminated from their body and energy fields, the aura becomes more and more translucent (lighter).

I believe the reason that Jesus' pictures were always painted with a halo is because people of the times actually saw the light emanating from his body.

Note: *The aura is not an indicator that one person is more spiritual than another. Everyone is perfect and in the right place on their spiritual journey. The aura is in a continuing state of change according to our emotions and experiences in the moment. Auric photographs can confirm changes that have taken place.*

✧   ✧   ✧   ✧   ✧

Jeffrey

It was Monday when our workshop sponsor entered the room accompanied by Jeffrey. She turned to us and asked, "Can you assist this man in a healing? He has serious problems and desperately needs your help."

"Our appointment calendar is completely booked," we replied.

Without hesitation, she countered, "Rich, cancel my appointment on Wednesday and put him in my place. He needs your help much more than I."

Jeffrey stepped forward and said, "I cannot wait till Wednesday. I am dying. I have just checked myself out of the hospital because they cannot find the cause of the problem and can do nothing for me. I am dying of my own toxins and will not last two more days. I have been unable to eat for five days."

We knew that Jeffrey was absolutely right. Calmly, with a reassuring smile, I replied, "Jeffrey, don't worry. We will do whatever is necessary to make sure that you are here for your appointment on Wednesday." With that, Ann Marie asked him to take a small amount of the *Harmonic Vibrational Essences* (see the chapter of that name on page 233) each hour to stabilize his life-force energy and reduce his stress. She also advised him that within a few hours he would be able to take small amounts of carrot juice and baby squash.

Tuesday morning had been scheduled with Dr. Ara Avedissian to complete a series of Kirlian photographs that would give scientific validation to some of our work.

Mid-morning of that day, Jeffrey burst into the room and pleaded, "You must do something now! I will not make it till tomorrow — I am dying!"

Once again I calmly assured him that we would do what was required to see that he would be able to keep his appointment the next afternoon. I placed my hand on his shoulder and said, "I can give you only a few minutes. I will do a short version of the Healing at this time. We will complete the two-hour appointment tomorrow. As long as you are here, would you be kind enough to have a Kirlian photograph taken to document your condition?"

"*Anything!*" he replied.

A photo was taken of the fingertips of one hand and the pad of one foot (see photos next page). Dr. Avedissian, using his knowledge from twenty-five years of medical research with Kirlian photography, began to translate what appeared on the pictures.

"Look at the shattered energy field of the middle finger. This represents your life-force energy. When that goes, you go. Now look at the foot. Notice the dark area under the second toe. This represents toxins that have accumulated in the body. Also note that there is a broken field of energy on each of the toes. Each toe represents a major organ, so this means that those organs are

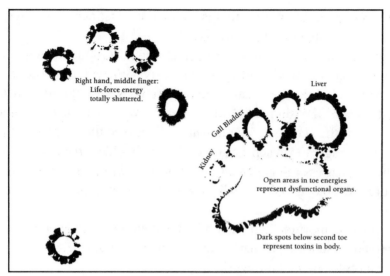

Jeffrey, first Kirlian photo.

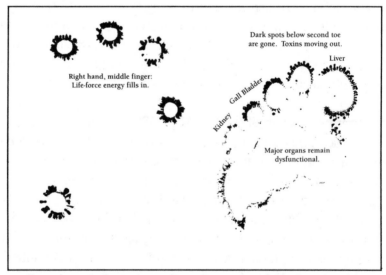

Jeffrey, second photo, same day; 15 minutes after taking six drops
Harmonic Vibrational Essences.

dysfunctional. That is why the toxins are building in the body." Looking at Jeffrey, he added, "You have serious problems."

Jeffrey acknowledged that he was already aware of that.

At this time Ann Marie asked Jeffrey to take six drops of Harmonic Vibrational Essences under his tongue, which would assist in raising his life-force energy and reducing his stress. Waiting fifteen minutes to allow his body to stabilize, we then asked the doctor to repeat the photographs (see second photo opposite)..

We noticed immediately that his life-force energy was restored and knew this would buy him more time to solve his other problems.

We asked Dr. Avedissian about the weak energy field of the foot. He reassured us that this was normal, as the energy was in the process of reestablishing itself. He added, "You will notice that the toxins were able to clear themselves; however, all of the major organs are still dysfunctional."

At this point I turned and asked Jeffrey to follow me into the next room where I could assist him in the Healing. Lying on the massage table, he displayed a great deal of anxiety over the seriousness of the problems he had been facing. "Jeffrey," I asked, "is it your desire to be well, whole and perfect in mind, body and soul?"

"Yes," he said firmly.

"I will do exactly what must be done at this time to assist you," I said. Tomorrow I will give you the full explanation of what we are doing today." We then began the Healing and the clearing of blocked energy fields. As I came to the liver, I intuitively sensed a serious blockage. Each time we tried to clear it, Jeffrey screamed in pain. It was as though we were physically ripping something from his body.

After three attempts, I asked Ann Marie to come in. "Look in the area of the liver and tell me what you see," I asked.

"There is a serious energy blockage in the liver area," she acknowledged.

"I know, but every time I try to remove it, he screams in pain," I explained.

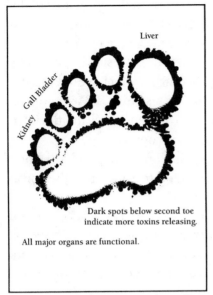

Liver

Gall Bladder

Kidney

Dark spots below second toe indicate more toxins releasing.

All major organs are functional.

Jeffrey, third photo, same day; after a 15-minute healing session.

Concentrating intensely, she said, "The energy is tied to the emotion *of terror*. Every time you try to remove it, he becomes so terrorized that he will not permit it to be removed."

Turning to Jeffrey, I said, "Do you understand what the rules are now?"

"Yes," he answered.

"Looking at him intently, I said firmly, "Do you choose to be free?"

"I choose to be free!" he said with conviction.

Once again I led him through the affirmation to release the blockage. He repeated each word as though his very life depended on it — and it did. With one final release of pain, it was over.

A few moments later we returned to the other room and asked Dr. Avedissian if he would take one more picture of the foot. Returning shortly with the third photo, the doctor excitedly said, "You will note that all the organs are now functional and that the toxins are being released."

The entire Healing had taken less than fifteen minutes. Jeffrey returned the next day for his two-hour appointment. We saw him several more times and Ann Marie instructed him on how to rebuild and nourish his depleted body. He was well on the road to recovery.

What could possibly have occurred in his life that would have created such a blockage, a condition that the medical profession was unable to diagnose and that threatened his very life? Fortunately, we were able to determine the cause.

Jeffrey had once joined an organization that he felt would empower him. (After all, isn't this what many of us are seeking, to reclaim our power?) However, he soon found that he was reciting rituals as part of this program. Instead of empowering *him*, without his knowledge they were insidiously placing *their* power over him. Although he was unaware of what was taking place, he later felt uncomfortable with this organization and decided to leave – and that was when his problems began.

I wonder how often something of this nature occurs that cannot be seen in an x-ray. Remember, there is nothing going on in the physical body that has not first occurred in the etheric (emotional) body.

> Here is how Webster defines ritual: "Consisting of ceremonials; a prescribed form or manner."

Brushing your teeth, taking a shower, driving the same way to work each day, can become a ritual. Anything that is repetitious, *including prayer*, can become a ritual. Words and thoughts are powerful, and actions are the result of thought. Choose your thoughts, words and actions carefully.

Not every Healing is as dramatic as those noted above, but if the intent is to receive a Healing, it will be received on many levels. The Healing cannot go beyond the point the person is prepared to accept. The person requesting the Healing is always in charge. Many who request a Healing have no major physical symptoms, but they realize there are emotional issues creating turmoil in their life and their relationships. If these emotional problems are left unresolved, the time will come when they will manifest into physical form.

The Master said,

"Ask and you shall receive."

He didn't say,

"Ask and we'll go have a committee meeting

and take a vote on it."

Do You Choose to Be Free?

If I were to put the healing process into a few words, it would be:

Whatever is interfering with my Free-Will Choice

or my ability to move forward in my life

according to my Heart's Desire,

I now choose to release.

There are many things that can interfere with free-will choice. The interfering energy that I refer to creates an imbalance in the polarities of our body and can be seen visually in our hands.

Place your hands together with the palms up and facing toward you like an open book. Line up your *heart lines* as shown in the picture. (It is the line that starts approximately 3/4 inch below your little finger and curves up toward your middle finger.)

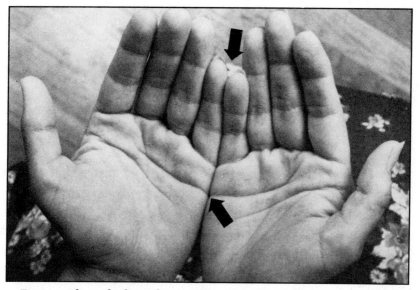

First match up the heart lines. Note: Knuckle creases do not match.

Let your eyes follow up your little fingers toward the fingertips. Check the creases on the inside of each knuckle on your little fingers. If the creases do not line up or if one of the little fingers appears longer than the other, you may have energies within your Being that are interfering with your free-will choice.

My question to you is, "*If there is anything interfering with your free-will choice, do you choose to be free?*"

If you choose to be free, I offer you the following affirmation to clear those interfering energies.

From the Divine Love that flows through my Being:

Whatever is in my auric field

that is interfering with my Free-Will Choice,

whether it is here with or without my permission,

I now command, in the name of the Creator

and from the Divine Love that flows through my Being

in Love and Peace,

that it now go to the Nucleus of its Being.

Go in Peace.

So be it!

Take a deep breath and let it go.

Check your hands again. Do the creases match? If so, the interfering energy has now been removed from your body.

If the creases do not line up, it is an indication that most likely (but not always) there is more than one soul in your body. I shall call them *entities*. If the creases on your little fingers line up after saying the affirmation in good faith, you can be sure any entities that were present are now gone.

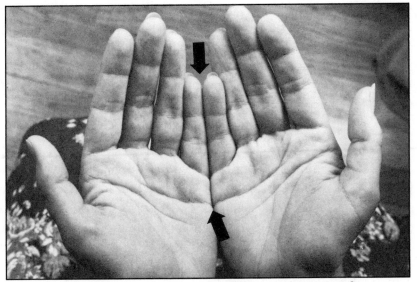

After Affirmation. Little fingers line up, creases match.

Each of us has free-will choice. When people die, they may choose to stay on Earth, but they do so without a body, and thus become Earthbound spirits.

We must understand that they are also part of God's wonderful creation, and when we ask them to leave, we do it with love. Everything we do is with love. You would not take a child, grab it by the scruff of the neck, open the door and say, "Get out of here," throwing it into the street. Like the child, the entity would say, "But this is my home. This is where I feel secure. What am I to do? Where am I to go?"

We chose to send it back to the *Nucleus of its Being*. The Nucleus of the Being is the spark that connects each one of us with the Creator.

There are many reasons for souls (entities) to be here on the Earth. Let me share a few with you.

I have heard a doctor comment that when he has a terminal patient, he will visit with that person for awhile. Then, almost as an afterthought, he will look directly into the person's eyes and say,

"You know, if you want to go, it's okay." He will then take a walk down the hall to get a cup of coffee, and as he returns and walks by that door, he looks in – and the patient is gone.

Imagine all the wonderful people who have a terminal illness. When the body gives out, some of these beautiful souls are still waiting for someone to say, "It's okay to leave."

✧　✧　✧　✧　✧

Let's take this a step further. We have a family in which the father has passed on. The wife is very much in love with him and misses him dearly. She manifests a disease so that she may cross over to meet him, but the children are holding on, saying, "Mom, don't leave us. You can't go." The mother is now caught in a tug-of-war between her guilt about leaving her children and her desire to leave. Finally, her body simply gives out, leaving her soul still tethered to the Earth. That emotional bond is greater than any rope that man could ever make.

✧　✧　✧　✧　✧

Or the time when a loving couple sat across from each other, sharing a romantic candlelight dinner. They raise their glasses of wine, look deeply into each other's eyes and say, "We'll be together forever."

Later one of them passes away and thinks, "I don't have to go anywhere. I have a contract here," and that soul enters the other's body.

They gave permission when they made the contract. Choose your words with care. Words are powerful, especially when said with conscious intent.

✧　✧　✧　✧　✧

Then there is the mother who loses a child and just can't let it go. She cannot bring herself to release the emotional bond and allow the soul to go on. That soul may feel its only option is to integrate with the mother. You now have a co-dependent relationship. As long as the soul of that loved one is not free to go onto its higher level of spiritual awareness, the mother is not free to exercise her own free-will choice.

✧   ✧   ✧   ✧   ✧

I refer to your body as your home, where no one can come in without your permission. But sometimes we give permission simply because we forget to close the door. When you are under anesthesia or in a coma, when you are ill or your energies are down, or when you've had a night out on the town with a little too much to drink, you are an ideal candidate for an entity to enter.

To have an entity is neither right or wrong. It is important to remember that the entity is not here to cause you harm. It is simply looking for a vehicle in which it can express itself. That's why you chose *your* vehicle — so that you could express yourself, to smell, taste, touch, and experience those things that a soul cannot do without a vehicle. To drink a glass of wine or taste a hot dog, you must have a body.

Sometimes an entity is content to sit in the back seat of your vehicle, just riding along and enjoying *your* experience. At other times it may say, "Get in the back seat. I want to drive for awhile." Later it might say, "Stay in the back seat. I like it up here," and you may find that you are no longer in charge of your vehicle. You may, in such a case, sense that you are carrying on a conversation with yourself. You say, "I believe I would like to go for a walk," and another voice says, "I would rather go have a drink."

✧   ✧   ✧   ✧   ✧

A lovely lady came to me and explained that her husband and son had both been killed in the same electrical accident. The son passed over without any problem; however, her husband was still here. She said, "I know he's here. There are a pair of his shoes in the closet. Every day I go to work and when I return home they are sitting by the front door. I put them back in the closet, and the next evening they will be by the front door." She added, "This is driving me crazy. I know he's here, but I don't know how to help him." I assisted her to let him go, using the simple affirmation shown earlier, and immediately she felt a sense of peace she had not known for a long time.

✧ ✧ ✧ ✧ ✧

Since everything in the universe is electromagnetic energy, including the soul, entities have a unique way of working with electricity. A gentleman who owned a tavern came to me for a private appointment and found to his surprise that he had an entity. I assisted him in releasing it. He looked at his hands in amazement, then said, "I own a tavern. I have a television mounted to the ceiling at the corner of the bar, and every time I turn it on, it shuts itself off. I turn it on again, and again it shuts itself off. I have had three separate repairmen check it out, and each one has told me there is nothing wrong with the TV set. Do you suppose there could be an entity in the bar?"

I replied, "They love bars. Those with psychic sight tell me that bars are full of entities just waiting for someone to lower their life-force energy so that they can enter and enjoy a drink. They love to party. Don't most people?"

Turning in his chair so that he could face me directly, he asked, "Would you come to my tavern and clear it?"

I smiled. "I will do better than that. I'm going to allow you to do it yourself. Distance is no object. Thought goes instantly to any point in all creation. It has no limitations. You can clear your place of business, your home, or any property that you own from the chair you are sitting in. What you may *not* do is try to "fix" the property of another. That would be interfering with *their* free-will choice. Just as you would not want someone to come into your home and start snooping around and rearranging your drawers, you do not have permission to invade another's property. There is a universal truth that you have heard before: "Whatever goes around, comes around." If you meddle, you will get meddled with. Assist another only when you have been asked.

"If you are prepared," I said, "I will guide you through the affirmation to clear your establishment."

He sat back, making himself comfortable in his chair. "I am ready," he said.

> *I call forth Archangel Michael*
>
> *to stand at the head of my property*
>
> *and Archangel Raphael to stand at the foot.*
>
> *I ask now that you spread your Golden Wings*
>
> *and sweep my property of any entities that are interfering*
>
> *with the Free-Will Choice of myself or my property,*
>
> *whether they are there with or without my permission.*
>
> *I ask that they now be removed by you,*
>
> *taken to the Nucleus of their Being,*
>
> *never to return.*
>
> *So be it!*

The gentleman called me two days later to tell me that his television set was now working perfectly.

✧   ✧   ✧   ✧   ✧

More than 50% of those who come to me for private appointments have an entity. Therapists who work with hypnotic regression are well aware this is not just an occasional occurrence. Some have told me that they believe that for every embodied human there are at least ten disembodied entities on the Earth at this time. They are simply Earthbound souls who have not cleared the Earth plane and gone to a higher level of spiritual awareness.

It is possible that as many as 90 to 95% of all entities can be cleared with the simple affirmation at the beginning of this chapter. If your fingers are still out of alignment, you may wish to consult someone experienced in exorcisms. Although it is possible that a person may simply have a deformed finger, you will find that in most cases it is an entity that is creating the disturbance in the energy field and the misalignment of the fingers.

Releasing these interfering energies is just one more step in reclaiming your mastery.

The Nucleus of the Being

is the spark that connects each one of us with the Creator.

The Cause of Disease

The cause of all disease and disharmony in your life is *emotional*.

Imagine, if you will, a pyramid. Its capstone represents disease. The layers of stone below represent pesticides, food dyes, chemicals, smoking, excess alcohol, job stress, marital stress — and the list goes on. The bottom layer of the pyramid symbolizes *emotions*. When you rake away the bottom layer, the pyramid collapses. There is no longer a foundation to support the disease.

There is nothing going on in your physical body that is not also going on in your emotional body. Your emotional body lies within your aura, the energy field that surrounds the body and is directly connected to the vibrations of every cell within it. When everything is in harmony within the emotional body, everything is in harmony within the physical body. When there is disharmony in the emotional body, that also is reflected in the physical body. As this disharmony increases, a diagnosable symptom develops in the physical body. Most therapies available today still focus on the symptom, not the cause of disharmony within the Being. When the disharmony is brought into alignment, into harmony, the symptom ceases. The foundation of the pyramid has been removed and the support for the capstone, disease, collapses. While it is possible for some therapies to trigger temporary remission of some symptoms, those symptoms will manifest again or appear in another form if the underlying cause has not been addressed. If the choice were yours, would you choose to keep patching the hole in the dam, or would you eliminate the need for the dam?

Heal your emotions and you will heal your body.

Toxic Metals

We have been exposed to many forms of toxic metals. It is a result of the modern society we live in. Many people are aware that they should not cook in aluminum pots and pans because microscopic flakes of aluminum from the cookware will be absorbed by the food and enter the body. Aluminum has been associated with Alzheimer's disease, among others.

We can also become exposed to excessive amounts of copper, iron and other metals. Research has shown that one of the metals most devastating to our health is mercury, which is one of the most toxic of all metals. Although we hear of excessive levels of mercury in rivers, lakes and oceans, our greatest exposure comes from the dental amalgams (combination of metals) used to fill our teeth. The euphemistic term for them is "silver fillings," but in reality they contain only a tiny amount of silver, plus zinc, tin, copper and approximately 50% mercury. Mercury is liquid at room temperature, and dentists use it because it makes a soft, pliable amalgam that can be easily worked into the small cavities in our teeth.

Many of us have, in our ignorance, held raw mercury in our bare hands in chemistry class. It is known that certain foods, supplements and acidic fluids such as coffee, tea and vinegar can release methyl mercury, which can enter the body and lodge in the cells, where it may stay until we do something to remove it. The body easily receives and stores toxic metals, but has little ability to remove them. When a recognizable symptom appears and is diagnosed as a disease, it is seldom associated with the accumulation of toxic metals.

Some diseases and symptoms associated with amalgam poisoning are cancer, leukemia, Hodgkin's disease, multiple sclerosis, arthritis, tachycardia (where the heart races over 200 beats per minute), angina and severe but unidentified chest pains, lupus, scleroderma, allergies (all types), chronic fatigue (a common symptom of amalgam poisoning), Crohn's disease, sickle-cell anemia, osteoporosis, ringing in the ears, slow healing, getting up at night to urinate – and this is only the beginning of a very long list. The documentation for the harmful effects of mercury poisoning is extensive.

I have stated before that chronic disease cannot exist in our body without an underlying emotional cause. This is true even when we have metals in our body. If an underlying emotional disharmony is not present, neither will disease be present. There are those who have a mouth full of fillings and experience no problems. Others may have a severe reaction to just one amalgam filling. Even if you were to remove all metal fillings, replacing them with nonmetallic materials, and remove excess metals from your blood and body tissues, those with underlying emotional disharmonies will still have those disharmonies. Toxic metals merely accelerate the manifestation of physical symptoms.

Metals are a low-vibration energy that interferes with the life-force energy of the body. The power of thought is the most powerful energy in the universe. Therefore it is possible to transmute the low-vibration materials into the higher vibration of *Universal Love* by repeating the following affirmation with proper intent.

All of our life we have been told all the things we cannot do. It is time that we remember all those things that we *can* do. Demonstrate it for yourself.

Ask a willing partner who has amalgam fillings: "Do you choose to have the toxic metal in your body made safe for you?" If he agrees, ask, "May I also include toxic residues?" (Toxic residues are anesthetics and other similar materials that can affect us.)

Then ask, "May I touch you?" After receiving his approval, have him raise his stronger arm, then muscle test for his normal strength, as described earlier in this book.

Now ask him to place the other hand's forefinger on a tooth that has an amalgam filling, placing it so that it touches both the tooth and the gum (on either the inside or the outside side of the tooth). While he holds his finger in this position, muscle test him again.

You will find his strength greatly reduced, indicating a dysfunction of energy. Then ask him to remove his finger from his mouth.

Now ask him to repeat aloud with you the following affirmation with you for transmuting toxic substances as you guide him through it line by line.

From the Divine Love that flows through my Being:

Surround my Soul with your Divine Light.

Allow now that your Divine Light,

your Light of Love,

your Light of Healing,

your Light of Protection,

your Light of Power and Wisdom,

become a permanent part of every molecule

of the toxic metals in my body

and all toxic residues

on all levels of my Being,

now and throughout my lifetime,

through all Time and Space and Beyond.

Allow now that they resonate

at the highest frequency of Unconditional Love.

Allow no negative thoughts or harmful energies to enter,

only the purest and the highest.

And no one shall change this affirmation

until I do so of my own Free-Will Choice.

So be it!

Ask him to place his finger on the tooth as before and muscle test again. You will find that not only is he strong, but most likely even stronger than before. The blessing is permanent, or until he chooses to change it of his own free-will choice.

The power of Prayer.

The power of Thought.

Letting Go

When you choose to release yourself from attachments
such as old bonds and dependent relationships
the space that separates
creates a void
waiting to be filled
with Unconditional Love

As you reconnect to the Dominions of Love
boundaries and limitations become restrictions of wholeness
walls of separation
impenetrable barriers of disconnection
leaving you to flounder aimessly through frustrations
and dramas of discontent
just out of reach of a solid foundation
and support from Universal Knowledge and Love

Removing all limitations
opens the door
to the adventure of receiving on all levels of your Being
the knowledge of your internal strength and power
and the wisdom that you and you alone control your destiny
allowing you to become all that you are
not having to learn
but simply to remember

The void within is filled with Love
Joy and Peace become the radiance of your Being
Harmony exists within each moment
You cannot work at being
in a state of Unconditional Love
it is merely the byproduct of letting go
and reconnecting to Love without conditions
You will no longer need dramas in your life
to serve as a catalyst to get you where you want to go
You will already be there

The Healing

If I could put "the Healing" in a few words, it would be:

Whatever is interfering with my Free-Will Choice

or my ability to move forward in life

according to my Heart's Desire,

I now choose to release.

This Healing has a beginning, a middle, an end and a purpose. As we move through the Healing, I will explain each part and share with you what each affirmation is intended to accomplish. The following is designed to take you step by step through a specific sequence of releasing energy patterns that have created undesirable bonds or attachments to yourself. To obtain the most beneficial results, please follow it in sequence.

Voicing affirmations without emotion or feeling does not get the job done. It is important that you use words that feel right to you. If at any time the words do not feel right, please select the appropriate words that do. It is not the words, but rather the *intent* of the words that you are choosing.

Those who work in interpersonal communication and understand body language know that people actually communicate from the solar plexus. When people place their arms over the solar plexus, they have just tuned you out. They are no longer receiving your message. In order to communicate freely, make sure that your arms do not interfere with the energy flowing from the solar plexus. Place them beside you on your lap, but away from the solar plexus.

After instructing one lady to place her arms at her side, I asked her, "How do you feel?"

She replied, "I feel very vulnerable."

I answered, "Yes, but in that vulnerability is the Healing, and in that vulnerability is your strength. It is in the letting go, the surrendering, that you will find the Healing you seek. It is time to let go of the control and start to allow. Stop *trying* and start *allowing*.

Take a few moments to reflect on what you are experiencing in your life that is not bringing you happiness and joy. Are you experiencing pain or discomfort? Are you experiencing emotional problems? Do you have fears? Do you have the prosperity that you desire at this time? Do you have someone to share your life with? If not, do you desire to have someone to share your life? What in your life do you desire to change? Make a list and review it carefully.

If those things you have listed are not bringing you happiness and joy, what is it you desire to change? Say it out loud. Before a change can take place, you must first make a commitment to change. Now write those words at the bottom of your list.

Before a change can take place,

you must first make a commitment to make a change in your life.

Declare Your Intent

It is not my intent to put thoughts into your head or words into your mouth. That would be interfering with your free-will choice. But I may offer you options: "Is it your desire to be Well, Whole and Perfect in mind, body and soul?"

If so, repeat with intent:

It is my desire to be Well, Whole and Perfect

in mind, body and soul.

(Following each affirmation throughout the book, take in a full, relaxing breath, inhaling through your nose, exhaling through your mouth, and feel Joy radiate from your heart to every part of your Being.)

You may choose to visualize it as taking in a "new breath of life" and letting go of "old energy patterns that have not brought you Joy."

Modern science tells us that we have approximately 100 trillion cells in our bodies, and you are much too busy to be worrying about what 100 trillion cells are doing every day. You have your work to do, schedules to keep, meals to make, and on and on. But you were smart enough to hire a General and to put the General in charge. You may know the General as the subconscious mind. The General has no sense of humor whatsoever. It will do anything you ask it to do. Interestingly enough, you are giving the General orders all day long, and if your orders happen to be, "I'm so sick of this job I could just die," the General turns around and says, "Well, guys, let's start wrapping things up. I guess he/she wants out of here." The cells literally start to shut down. But if your orders of the day are, "It is my desire to be well, whole and perfect in mind, body and soul," it turns around and says, "Come on, guys, let's get busy. We're going on a grand adventure."

Science has also documented what appears to be the existence of the soul in the physical body. Scientists took a group of people who were about to expire and asked if they could weigh them at the moment of death. The group agreed, and it was discovered that the average person loses between 11 and 13 ounces at the moment of death.

Although some may not think of it in this manner, everyone in the profession of healing truly wants to accomplish one thing: to open a free flow of energy throughout your Being so everything will begin to work properly again.

The intent of this Healing is no different. It simply offers you different tools.

Imagine that you have a hose hooked up to the faucet at the side of your house. You turn on the faucet and pick up the end of the hose, but there's no water coming out. You inspect the hose carefully and find that there is a kink in the middle. You know that if you ignore the kink and keep the water pressure turned on, it could develop a bulge and might even burst. This is what happens in our Being. If there is a blockage in our Being, as energy flows in and the pressure begins to build, we soon get discomfort, pain, and other symptoms of disharmony. When that blockage is removed, everything begins to flow.

✧ ✧ ✧ ✧ ✧

Several years ago a wonderful lady called and stated that because she was unable to travel to me, she wanted me to come to her farm to assist her in her Healing. It was Friday night and I had no other commitments for the weekend, so I drove the forty miles. Upon arriving, I found several people sitting around the kitchen table. My hostess' first words were, "How many of us can you do?"

I asked, "How many do you have?" I was expecting one Healing.

She replied, "There are ten of us."

I said, "I couldn't possibly complete all ten in one evening, but if you have a room for me to stay overnight, I will finish up tomorrow morning."

Each one of these people were involved in healing work in one form or another, yet as I worked with them, I found that each had a disease, aches, pains and/or emotional problems. I realized that all these wonderful people had come forth as my teachers, to make me aware that even those who assist others in their healing still had healing of their own to complete.

I always see the person before me as my teacher, and I am always the student. Sometimes they come to validate the tools I use. Other times they bring new challenges for which I must go inside and find new tools. As each one came forth, I related to them the story about the hose, and then shared the lesson I had received.

✧ ✧ ✧ ✧ ✧

I had reached a point of extreme stress in my life. Adding to the stress in my personal life, I had involved myself in books, workshops and meditations to open my own spiritual journey. It was then that I received a message from a valued friend. "Rich," he said, "I strongly suggest that for the next thirty days you do not meditate or listen to a spiritual tape, read a spiritual book or go to a workshop. Go get an entertaining novel and get grounded. You are on spiritual overload."

Many of us get on our spiritual pathway and we don't want to miss graduation day. We can't read enough or do enough. We do not take time to honor ourselves. The source of the stress does not matter. Stress is stress. If we have a blockage and the energy continues to flow in, the results and the symptoms are the same. Take time to rest. Take time to play. Honor the beautiful creation that you are.

Stress from any source is stress.

✦ ✦ ✦ ✦ ✦

God has a box of hammers of all sizes. There may come a point in one's life when God takes out a little hammer and goes tap, tap, tap and says, "Can you hear me?"

Some may reply, "Shoo, shoo, go away, I'm busy."

Later God uses a bigger hammer: Knock, knock, knock. "Can you hear me now?"

Again they answer, "Don't bother me. I'm much too busy."

Finally, God takes out a two-by-four and whacks them up the side of the head and says, "Can you hear me *now*?"

Lying on their sickbed, facing some serious decisions in their life, they reply, "I believe I can. What are you trying to tell me?"

Sometimes we get caught up in the quicksand of the lesson and we don't know how to get out. When this occurs, we begin to develop symptoms. It is the body's way of telling us that we now have a choice to make. It is *your* lesson and only you can decide if you wish to stay put or move beyond it. Neither choice is right or wrong; it is simply a choice. Focus not on the lesson, but rather on the *value* received from the lesson. How have you benefited? How have you grown?

✦ ✦ ✦ ✦ ✦

The following affirmation will give direction to all affirmations that you will say throughout your journey.

Affirmation to Prepare to Receive Healing

From the Divine Love that flows through my Being:
It is my intent that all Affirmations
that I say this day
and each day,
reflect through all Time and Space and Beyond
and on all levels of my Being.
I now call forth the Nucleus of my Being,
the very Core of my Wholeness,
to integrate with me in Unconditional Love,
in Mind, Body and Soul,
to accept this Healing.
So be it!

✦ ✦ ✦ ✦ ✦

The Child Within

Many today recognize the term "the child within." We refer to them as *fragments of our Being.* We are a complex Being of mind, body and spirit. Remember that the physical body is only a reflection of what is going on in the energy (etheric) body.

Imagine that when you were a child someone said to you, "You know something? You are never going to grow up to amount to anything!"

Your reaction would be, "Ouch, that hurts!" A fragment of your emotional body has been wounded and now withdraws and surrounds itself in a cocoon of protective energy where it will feel safe and secure.

Later another playmate teases you by saying, "Not only that, your clothes are ugly, too!" That hurts, too. Now another fragment of your emotional body pulls back and surrounds itself in a cocoon of safety. When we take into consideration the totality of all that we are at all levels of our being and at all levels of consciousness, we have, not a few fragments of our Being, but thousands of them.

The reason that most do not receive the Healing they desire is that not all of them are fully present for the Healing. As the person leaves to go for his Healing, the fragments are saying, "You go and have a good time. We'll be here when you get home." Later, some of the fragments will say, "Gee, I think I'll try that, too," and several more participate. This process could go on indefinitely.

We thank those who have brought to our consciousness the fact that there is a child within. Before any Healing can truly have a long-term effect, we must first integrate the totality of our Being, so it can participate in wholeness in the Healing.

The following affirmation will lovingly invite all those fragments to come together and to participate as one in the Healing.

Affirmation to Integrate All Aspects of Being

From the Divine Love that flows through my Being:

I call forth all aspects of my Being

that are tethered to the Earth

to stand before me

as I stand before you – in Love.

I ask you now to integrate with me in Unconditional Love.

I call forth all aspects of my Being

to stand before all other aspects of my Being.

I ask you now to forgive all aspects,

to accept forgiveness,

and to release all bonds between you

except that of Unconditional Love.

I ask you to join me now as I embrace you in Love

to move through all time.

I now call forth the fragments of my Being, joyfully united,

to move through all time in Peace and Harmony.

So be it!

I used to say only the last part of this affirmation, until I had a person before me in which there was something we could not bring into harmony.

Looking within for the answer, I realized that one fragment had not participated, that it was itself fragmented into even smaller aspects, and when we called the fragments forth, it in effect would say, "That doesn't include me, I'm not whole."

I asked the person before me, "Tell me once again about your life."

She had left a long-term marriage in which her husband had not taken her on a honeymoon and had rarely taken her to a party or enjoyed a vacation together. The few social engagements they did have were occasional dinners with friends. If she was having a good time, her mate thought something must be wrong and let her know it. She soon found that "it hurt to have a good time." She also found that if she agreed with her husband, she was always right, but if she did not, she was always wrong. She found that "it hurt to speak her truth."

When she entered another relationship, her new partner told her this relationship would be based on "unconditional love." "The door swings both ways," he said, "and it swings in love." If you feel at any time you need to leave to further your growth, you may do so in love, and with my blessings." She entered into that relationship, but every time she said something, she said it with caution, looking over her shoulder to see if she was going to be chastised. This was scary. It was new territory, and she didn't know what the rules were.

I explain this as having a dog on a leash. The dog is a real tiger, tugging at the leash because it knows where its boundaries are. Suddenly the leash breaks and the dog lunges forward. Startled, it looks around and says, "Oh-oh, I've never been here before. I don't know what the rules are; put me back on the leash."

Several times she thought of going back into the old relationship because she knew what the rules were. She explained that each time she and her new friend would go out to have a good time, she would end up crying.

I interrupted my client. "Why were you crying?"

She thought for a moment, and then realized, "Because it hurts to have a good time."

"What did we miss?" I questioned. It was then that we found that one or more fragments had not participated. Then I added the first half to the affirmation, and had her repeat the entire affirmation once again. The shattered fragment was made whole and accepted the Healing. Now she can go out and have a good time. Remember, every vibration of your Being has a consciousness and a memory.

✧　✧　✧　✧　✧

Wired with Interfering Energies

There are many energies interfering with our free-will choice. Our universe is one of energy. You are an energy Being made up of cells, molecules and atoms that are pure energy. There are many disrupting energies on the Earth at this time. In many cases man has created powerful electronic devices for his own purpose without thought as to how it might affect the human body — microwave stations, radar, powerful ELF (extra-low frequency) devices, towers sending radio and television signals, to name a few. Some of these energies can be very detrimental to the human experience and life in all forms.

When these energies distort the energy field that surrounds our body (the aura), stresses and dysfunctions are created in the total Being, including the emotional body. This may be expressed first as emotional problems, but ultimately will be reflected as symptoms in our physical body.

✧　✧　✧　✧　✧

The Shadow of Fear

One day I turned to Ann Marie and said, "Now that we have learned how to assist those who desire to be unwired from interfering energies, a new teacher will come forth. The next day I made a phone call to a person I had assisted recently in a Healing. She was trembling as she spoke on the phone. I asked, "What is going on?"

She replied, "I feel as if someone is trying to take control of my body, and I'm afraid that its going to win. I have this incredible *fear* surrounding me."

I turned to Ann Marie and said, "We have our new teacher. Let's find the underlying cause." We brainstormed throughout the evening, and by morning I knew that we had the final parts to our answer.

Of the many powerful and disturbing electromagnetic energies in the Earth's atmosphere at this time, there are certain frequencies that are directly interfering with the higher vibrational energies, or the frequencies of Love. They are creating a distortion of light in the human aura which amplifies the *emotion of fear*.

The frequency of Love may be perceived as pure rays of light, whereas fear is perceived as distorted rays of light. In the human aura, these distortions create shadows in the energy field.

I soon became aware of three other individuals I had recently assisted with their Healing, who were now beginning to display the same symptoms of fear. As Ann Marie and I looked at these people collectively, they all appeared to have one thing in common. They all had a dark cloak of energy around them, which we now refer to as the *Shadow of Fear*.

I asked one of them if she would be kind enough to undergo hypnotic regression, and she agreed. During the session the hypnotherapist asked her to call forth the Shadow of Fear.

Momentarily she said, "I can see the Shadow now, and it is angry."

She was told to ask it to come forth in clarity all the way.

After a short pause, she stated, "I can see him now, and he is really angry."

Finally she was directed to ask, "What name do you answer to?"

A moment went by, then she said, "The God of Fear."

Her statement was more profound than would appear at first glance. We have discovered that anyone who has chosen or acknowledged and accepted an organization, society, group or individual whose values were based on fear, has in effect accepted the God of Fear. This connection leads to a separation from Source (the Creator), creating a "shadow," or cloak of distorted light within the aura. This shadow is further being amplified at this time by the interfering electromagnetic frequencies that are present in the Earth's atmosphere. The more people try to raise their vibrations of Love when fear and judgment are present, the more it creates a greater distortion of light in their aura. The result is chaos.

The more you try to raise your vibrations to the higher vibrations of Love, the more resistance you experience. It has been interfering with your free-will choice and your ability to fully express the gift you have brought here to share. You try to bring Love into your life, but you create fear instead. You try to manifest prosperity, but you create poverty. You try to create a business and the phone doesn't ring. It isn't fun anymore, thus many people feel they just want to leave.

For some, life can become so frustrating and chaotic, they become suicidal. One person said, "My life is falling apart before my eyes. Every relationship I have is suddenly at odds; my dogs no longer recognize me, and in fact run from me. My business has stopped completely. Life isn't fun anymore. I just want out."

We do not have to look far to find those who are experiencing a great amount of fear in their life.

At this time I would share with those who choose to be free, the following affirmation that will release the bonds of the "wiring" and the Shadow of Fear.

My question to you: *If there is anything interfering with your free-will choice, do you choose to be free?* If so, complete the following affirmation.

Removing Interfering Energies and the Shadow of Fear

From the Divine Love that flows through my Being:
Whatever laws I have owned,
whatever beliefs I may hold,
whatever vows I have made,
whatever contracts or agreements I have made
and those I have made them with —
through all Time and Space and Beyond
and on all levels of my Being —
that have created these judgments within my Being
that are not bringing me Happiness and Joy,
Now, of my own Free-Will Choice,
I release.
Goodby and God bless.

I now call forth the Angels of Divine Perfection
to assist me in restoring myself
and my property, past, present and future,
and the Elementals attached to that property,
all to its Divine Perfection.

I call forth the Shadow of Fear,

including all laws, judgments and fears relating to it,

as well as all property that I own, past, present and future,

to stand before me now as I stand before you – in Love.

I ask you now to forgive me as I forgive you.

I thank you for the lessons that we have shared.

I now choose to release all bonds between us

except for those of Unconditional Love.

I now choose to transmute

those laws, judgments, fears and property

into Unconditional Love.

I bid you to go in Peace.

So be it!

Your property is an extension of yourself. Your glasses, your watch, clothes, car, your real estate, are extensions of who you are, and any energy that affects you also affects your property. If the person that you acquired your property from was affected by negative or undesirable energies, including illness, that energy is still present in the property. This affirmation addresses those properties, past, present and future. Any property that you choose to purchase or move into, has now been cleared and is free to manifest more readily into your life.

✧   ✧   ✧   ✧   ✧

Relationship Entities

Each of us is an individual entity (mind, body and soul). Whenever you are with another person, you form a collective energy field that we call a *relationship entity*. Each time you form a new relationship with a friend, fellow employees or any individual or group of persons, you form another relationship entity, and we do this many times throughout the day. Entities attached to others can enter into these energy fields and interfere in our relationships. This also interferes with our free-will choice.

The following affirmation will free you from this interference.

Affirmation to Remove Interfering Relationship Entities

From the Divine Love that flows through my Being:

Whatever is in my auric field

and the auric fields of my relationships –

with individuals, with groups,

with the Earth, with the Universe and with the Creator,

and on all levels of my Being,

through all Time and Space and Beyond –

that is interfering with my Free-Will Choice,

whether it is here with or without my permission,

I now command, in the name of the Creator

and from the Lord God of my Being

in Light and Love,

that it now go to the Nucleus of its Being.

Go in Peace.

So be it!

❖   ❖   ❖   ❖   ❖

Other Interfering Energies

There are other energies that can interfere with our free-will choice. These areas will be included together in one beautiful, flowing affirmation.

Control Devices: Control devices are self-explanatory. When we consider the complex beings that we are, in mind, body and spirit, it's hard to find anyone who does not have some kind of control that has been placed on them. To heal it, it's not necessary to know its source. We are simply saying, "If there is anything interfering with my free-will choice and my ability to move ahead on my spiritual journey, I now choose to release it."

Severed Parts: If you were to use Kirlian photography to take photos of the energy field of an amputee, the photograph would show the energy field of that person complete, with the limb still intact. The same is true if you had an organ removed or any part of your physical body altered. The energy field is still present; however, there may be disruption in the flow of the auric energy that reflects a disharmony in the physical body. (Remember the amputee whose toes still itched?)

When we call forth those parts that have been altered in any form to be reunited in divine perfection, many physical pains may improve or simply go away.

The Umbilical Cord of Life: A beautiful young lady came forth as my teacher. She was studying to be a concert musician, and then her extroverted personality changed to one of total introversion.

She found it uncomfortable to be in the same room with someone else. If the phone rang, she would panic. Being alone in the room with me for a Healing was a major step for her. But at the end of the Healing, everything was just fine. It was a wonderful experience. Everything was fine except for *one* thing: She said, "Rich, can you do something for my back?"

I asked her to roll over so I could take a look. As I touched her lightly on the back, her entire body went into spasms. I said, "What is it that we have here?"

Finally able to calm herself, she replied, "I don't know, but I've had it for some time."

Ann Marie was through with her appointments, so I asked her to join me. I then touched the young woman's back one more time, with the same result. Turning to Ann Marie, I said, "Let us focus on the underlying cause."

A moment passed, then Ann Marie said, "Focus on the umbilical cord."

"Of course," I said, now understanding. "The umbilical cord of the physical body has been severed, but the cord of the etheric body is still attached to your mother, your grandmother, your children and your grandchildren, if you have any."

Everyone understands the emotional bond a mother has for her child. The child could be halfway around the world, but if it stubs its toe, the mother goes "ouch!" We are suggesting that there may be times when we experience some things that we do not fully understand at the conscious level. Imagine, if you will, how many may have said, "Mother, if I could, I would take on your pain for you." Mother may have thought, "Sounds like a heck of a deal to me! You can have it *all.*"

Since that time I have had clients who have done exactly that. One client said, "Rich, I've really got a problem. My elderly mother is in a health-care home, and every time she has a toothache, I have a toothache; every time she stubs her toe, my toe aches. This has been driving me crazy. Can you help me?" I knew I could, because my teacher had now come forth.

The affirmation below for the Umbilical Cord is the one I offered the young lady — and her problem was gone.

Affirmations to Remove Other Interfering Energies

I call forth Archangel Michael to stand at the head of my Soul,
and Archangel Raphael to stand at the foot.
I ask now that you spread your Golden Wings
and surround my Soul with Light, Love and Protection.
I ask now:
Anything that is interfering with my Free-Will Choice —
whether it has been placed there with or without my permission,
be it thought forms, monitors, restrictions, bindings,
anything at any level of my Being
through all Time and Space and Beyond
and on all levels of my Being —
Remove it now, take it to a place of your choosing
and dispose of it according to your will, never to return.

I also call forth anything that has been severed or altered
in any form, at any level of my Being
through all Time and Space and Beyond,
to be reconnected and aligned in Divine Perfection,
for I now choose to be whole.

At this time I ask that the Umbilical Cord of Life
that attaches my Soul to all other Souls now be brought forth,
and any darkness that lies within the Umbilical Cord of Life
also be called forth to be Loved and Honored,
for it has served me well in my journey.
But I now choose to be Well, Whole and Perfect
in Mind, Body and Soul,
And I choose to replace that darkness
with the pure Light of Unconditional Love,
to be enfolded once again into my Being
as I now move forward in my journey.

I thank you, Archangels Michael and Raphael,
for your loving presence.
I bid you to go in Peace, and ask only that you leave with me
the essence of your Love and your Protection
to surround my Soul as I move forward in my journey.
So be it!

✧ ✧ ✧ ✧ ✧

The Seven Chakras of the Body

"Chakra" is a Sanskrit word denoting energy centers. We will address the seven major chakras of the body. Chakras are often described by the different colors they represent. I will refer to them in a different manner.

Emotions are the underlying cause of all chronic disease. And there are only two basic emotions — *love* and *fear*. Then there are the derivative emotions, which are known as joy, security, trust, peace, harmony, tranquility, jealousy, anger, rage, hate, etc. Each emotion relates to a different chakra or part of our body. Each chakra has a different frequency. Each organ and part of the body also has a different frequency. If you were to tell me that you were having liver problems, I would ask you what you were "angry" about. If you were having a gall bladder attack, I would ask, "What are you in 'rage' about?" The underlying emotional cause of cancer is *suppressed anger*. The cancer's location reveals another emotional disharmony the person is dealing with. Release your fears and you will release your disease.

❖   ❖   ❖   ❖   ❖

There is the proverbial ninety-year-old man who smokes a box of cigars a day, enjoys his drinks, stands on the street corner, vents his anger, hasn't seen a doctor in fifty years and is the picture of health.

Then there is the grandmother who has never ever used a four-letter word, eats all the right foods, has never missed Sunday services — and yet she has developed disease. If you were to go back into her life, you might find that she had been an abused child, but being a proper young lady, as society expected her to be, she had stuffed her anger and said, "I'll deal with it in my own way." At the conscious level she is probably unaware that this emotion still exists.

A long time ago you made a contract with your subconscious mind. It said, "Look, I'll take all the garbage you want to give me and I'll store it for as long as you want, but sooner or later you have to pay the rent." Someday the rent will come due.

Chakra #1 – From Pelvis to Foot (Self-Judgment): The area from the pelvis to the bottom of the feet is called the "root chakra." It includes the sexual organs, hips, legs, knees etc. This chakra deals with *laws and judgments.* The vibration of judgment goes right to the hips. If someone is having hip pain, sciatic nerve problems, or needing a hip transplant, their condition has been created by their judgments.

Do you remember what Jesus said we must become in order to enter the kingdom of heaven? "As little children." It was so simple that many missed his message. Little children have no laws except for the one from the Creator, the *Law of Free-Will Choice.* You can go up, you can go down, you can go left or right, you can go bang your head on the wall and find that it brings you pain, or you can go· outside and play and find that it brings you joy. Simply different choices, no judgment. One day your mother says, "No, dear, you can't go outside the back yard." Later you sneak out of the back yard, thinking, "Oh, oh, I just broke one of Mommy's rules [laws]. If she catches me, she's going to be angry [judge me]. She may even punish me." It wasn't a bad law, for it was done out of love and a desire to protect you.

Then you went to school and the teacher said, "If you do such-and-such, you'll be punished." So you bought into more laws just just so you could get through the day. Society had already hung some heavy expectations on you by the time you found that the government can't seem to write laws fast enough. In some of your relationships, you may have found you bought into some *laws* just so you could get through the day.

I put it this way: When you do something for someone that brings you joy, it's wonderful. If two people do something for each other that brings them both joy, it's absolutely beautiful. But if you do something for someone that does *not* bring you joy, I suggest that you take two steps back and ask, "Why did I do this? It did not bring me joy."

We all jump into the river of life. Many of us begin to swim upstream, and after awhile we say, "You know, I've been swimming a long time. I'm sure getting tired and don't seem to be getting anywhere." Then someone on the riverbank shouts, "Hey, dummy, turn around and go with the flow." We are here to learn how to go with the flow. To let go and let God. To put our thoughts into Universal Consciousness, reinforced by desire, then step aside and allow the universe to manifest it for us. To stand in our Mastery. "Ask and ye shall receive," the Master said.

There was a time in your life when someone asked, "Is that you?"

"No, that's not me" was the reply. You held up a cardboard image and said, "This is what society expects me to be, so this is who I will pretend to be." Behind that cardboard image, in the closet with the door closed and the light turned out, is a frightened child, afraid that someone will open the door and turn on the light. The interesting thing is, here is a cardboard image talking to all these *other* cardboard images, because the others are playing the same game. They are trying to live their life as society or their friends or their relatives want them to. Many are living their life for everyone else except themselves. They are living *The Lie*.

If you do something for someone and that action is not bringing you joy, you are swimming upstream. The affirmation that follows is part of one that was said earlier.

To deny your identity (your Truth) is to live The Lie.

Affirmation to Release Laws and Judgments

From the Divine Love that flows through my Being:
Whatever laws I have owned,
whatever beliefs I may hold,
whatever vows I have made,
whatever contracts or agreements I have made
and those I have made them with —
through all Time and Space and Beyond
and on all levels of my Being —
that have created these judgments within my Being
that are not bringing me Happiness and Joy,
Now, of my own Free-Will Choice,
I release.
Goodby and God bless.
So be it!

✧   ✧   ✧   ✧   ✧

Chakra #2 – From Pelvis to Navel (Fears): The digestive system is the *fear* chakra. Everyone can relate to this. When we have fear, we feel a knot in our gut. You can eat all the right foods, but your fears will take those good foods and turn them into chemical poisons. Somebody says, "It all has to do with diet, doesn't it?" Well, it's a good place to start.

Medical writings have documented cases where nursing mothers were experiencing intense anger, and the child would die within an hour; other infants experienced severe toxicity from the poisons in their mother's milk.

You cannot fear anything you've never experienced before on one level of consciouness of another. For example, a young child who sees a beautiful candle for the very first time says, "My, that's pretty," sticks its finger into the flame, and exclaims, "Ouch, that burns!" The next time it sees a flame, it will take two steps back. If you have never been raped on one level of consciousness or another, you have no fear of walking down a dark street at night. Fear is only your teacher. It reminds you that you have done this one before.

On the other hand, the Creator says, "You have to do your lessons only once." There is no value going through the same class three or four times, but you do have free-will choice, and if you choose to do that, that's okay, too.

My suggestion is, when you experience a fear, simply acknowledge to yourself silently or aloud (it is the intent that counts) in whatever words you choose in the moment: "I've done this before and I choose not to do it again."

You will not have to do it again. The Creator will not let you.

Allow me to share some experiences others have had. Each of them had come for private appointments.

✧   ✧   ✧   ✧   ✧

A lady phoned a few days after her appointment. "Rich," she exclaimed excitedly, "I just had to call and share this with you. I went to a workshop the other night, and when it was over I went to the dimly lit parking lot to get my car. As I reached in my purse to get my keys, two men stood up on the other side of my car and began to approach me. Fear ran through me because I knew what their intent was, but I remembered to say, "I've done this before and I choose not to experience it again!" She added, "Rich, I no sooner said that than they both stopped dead in their tracks. They looked at each other, then looked around as if to say, "What am I doing here?"

"I got in my car," she continued, "and as I drove away, I looked back and the two men were stumbling around as if they were lost in a fog."

✧ ✧ ✧ ✧ ✧

This beautiful lady had been married to an alcoholic. When he was sober, he was very nice, but when he wasn't, he would use her for a punching bag. One night he came home quite intoxicated, found a baseball bat, and chased her around the house with the drunken intent of beating her brains out. She ran up the stairs, screaming for her life, but got cornered in the hallway, with noplace to go. "Rich," she said, "as he raised the bat, I shouted, 'God, protect me!' and in that moment I became very calm, realizing that he could not hurt me. I simply stood there and watched him as the bat came down again and again. It was as if someone had placed a plexiglass wall between us; he could not complete the swing of the bat. Finally, he threw the bat on the floor in frustration, went downstairs and passed out." She added, "I packed my bags and left."

✧ ✧ ✧ ✧ ✧

A business man, dressed in a suit and carrying a briefcase, was walking down the streets of Philadelphia at night. Out of the corner of his eye he saw an old car pacing him. Soon the car pulled up ahead and stopped, and five rough-looking young men jumped out and surrounded him. A couple of them were holding switchblade knives. Crouching, swaying from side to side, they chanted, "We're gonna get ya, buddy, we're gonna get ya!" Looking at the young men with indifference, the businessman just stood there, then turned and walked right between two of them. He said, "They had to know I left, because I brushed shoulders with them. I walked across the street, then turned to look back. As I stood looking across the street at where I had been," he continued "all five were still in a circle, crouched and chanting, 'We're gonna get ya, buddy, we're gonna get ya." He said, "Rich, I could see no one inside the circle." A few moments later he heard one say, "Oh, the hell with him, let him go," and they got back into the car and drove away.

When you stand in your Divine Perfection

in Unconditional Love, without fear,

there is no one more powerful than you.

✧   ✧   ✧   ✧   ✧

There is nothing you can *do* to be who you are. You already *are* who you are. There is no workshop you can attend, no book you can read, no tapes you can listen to, no meditation you can do, no society you can join. You *already are* who you are. You need only reach out and remove the veils of illusion that have been placed around you. You are the Divine Creation. Simply allow yourself to be who you are.

If you step back into fear, you will open Pandora's box and all the other possibilities that fear can create. When you choose to stand in Unconditional Love, you will be tested. A teacher will come forth and say, "Come on, let's test this person and find out if he's only saying that — or does he really mean it?"

It is one thing to understand Unconditional Love,

It is another to live it.

You have come here to be the Master that you are; to stand in your truth, in Unconditional Love — a state of being without judgment.

Conditional Love creates drama in your life.

Unconditional Love takes you out of the drama.

We find ourselves being tested frequently when we choose to walk the path of Unconditional Love. Ann Marie and I chose to stand in our truth, and intuitively knew we would be tested.

I was in Louisville, Kentucky, driving the motor home and towing an automobile on a multiple-lane street. I had to move over one more lane to make a left turn. Looking in my rear-view mirror, I saw that the lane to my left was clear for about six car lengths. I switched on my turn signal and slowly started to pull over. As soon as I did, a car that was several car lengths back stepped on the gas, moving quickly to my left side. This upset me. I clenched my teeth and began to crowd the car. The other driver was also determined not to give way. Still not happy with someone who was so inconsiderate, I moved even closer. Ann Marie shouted, "Careful, you're going to hit them." Then Ann Marie began to laugh uncontrollably and said, "You don't suppose you're being tested, do you?" Immediately I burst out laughing and thought, Oh, no. As soon as I laughed, the car sped away as if it had never been there in the first place.

A few days later we were driving along the West Virginia Turnpike in the car. Ann Marie said jokingly, "Let me drive the car. You know how you get." It had been snowing, and although there was enough snow to plow, it was not so deep that experienced drivers could not handle it. Ahead of us were two snowplows side by side going 15 miles per hour. There was no reason they could not have gone 45 to 55 miles per hour, and certainly there was no reason to travel side by side. Cars began stacking up behind them. As time progressed, Ann Marie was getting angrier and her face became flushed. For twenty minutes the snowplows kept the traffic blocked. Finally, unable to contain herself any longer, she looked at me in total frustration and said, "Teach me how to do the finger."

I roared with laughter. Finally, controlling myself long enough to get my voice, I replied, "You don't suppose you're being tested, do you?"

"Oh my God!" she exclaimed, bursting out in laughter. The moment she began laughing, one snowplow pulled ahead of the other and let the cars go by.

You will be tested, but as you demonstrate that you can *live your truth*, the testing will subside.

Unconditional Love: A State of Being without Judgment.

Affirmation to Release Fears

From the Divine Love that flows through my Being:
Whatever fears I may have,
I know I have experienced them before.
And since I have known them before,
I choose not to experience them again.
I now choose to forgive all my fears
and all my reactions to those fears.
So be it!

✧   ✧   ✧   ✧   ✧

Chakra #3 — From Navel to Bottom of Rib Cage (Power): This is heavy-duty territory. It includes the adrenals, kidneys, liver, gall bladder, pancreas, stomach and spleen. It is the *power* chakra. In order to enter the kingdom of heaven we must become as a little child. Little children have no laws, and they have total power over their creations. We love little children because they are not buying into everything we tell them. They are free spirits. We would love to emulate them, but if we did, we'd be put in a padded room. After awhile we give children some laws and settle them down. When Mother said, "No, dear, you can't leave the back yard," you not only accepted a law, you also gave up some of your power. Society/government would like to have much of your power, and friends and relatives would like to have what is left over. Have you ever noticed how many people want to tell you how to run your life? Those who choose to play the game of *power and control* know the rules well:

> If I can keep you in these *Laws,*
>
> If I can keep you in these *Fears,*
>
> If I can keep you in this *Power,*
>
> If I can keep you from *Loving yourself —*
>> Just one of these — I can *control* you.
>>
>> *All* of them — I can *own* you.

Their greatest fear is that *you* may learn how to play the game too, because when you do, they can no longer control you.

✧　✧　✧　✧　✧

With your permission, I would like to take you on a beautiful visual journey.

Walk with me, if you will, down this beautiful, old-time street. It is a lovely street. We come to an old-fashioned theater. We open the door and walk inside. The stage is huge, and we climb up onto the stage and go to the middle. Now, for a moment I'm going to walk off the stage, leaving you standing there by yourself. Soon you see yourself removing yourself from your body. You see yourself going into the audience and finding a comfortable seat high up where you can see the entire stage below, with yourself standing in the middle.

People begin walking onto the stage, and soon it is completely full of people. As you are watching this beautiful scene unfold, you realize that all of these people are all of those people you've had a relationship with in any form in this lifetime.

There's Mom and Dad. Your siblings. All your relationships. Yes, there's the doctor, the baker, and the candlestick maker. All of them are there. As you watch this scene unfold, you also become aware that before these beautiful souls came to this Earth stage they all sat in a celestial realm, drinking a glass of celestial wine and discussing, what is it like to eat a hot dog; to smell the roses; to be angry.

"I don't know," says one. "You need a body to experience those things."

Another says, "Look, I'll tell you what: I'll be the mother, and you can be the father. Later we can have a child, and you can be our child."

At that time they decide what life experiences they will share when they come here. They also agree to work together as long as necessary and in whatever manner necessary to bring forth the values of the lessons they have chosen.

Once again looking onto the stage below, you realize the stage is empty. You become aware that once again these beautiful souls have returned to that celestial realm to share another glass of wine and discuss, What of value did we bring from this incarnation? It wasn't the lesson; it wasn't the life experience – that's just old baggage, and we have no room for that baggage. What of value did we bring that would raise the vibration of the soul in its service to its Creator? Did we learn to release our laws, to release our fears? Did we reclaim our power and acknowledge love for the divinity within? These are the things that raise the vibration of the soul.

Once again, sitting in the audience looking on the empty stage below, you suddenly realize that there is no blood on the stage: there are not even any dead bodies. The only thing left is a giant screen scrolling the cast of characters: "This one played the mother, that one played the father, and I played myself."

In the following affirmation we are going to declare that we love and honor those who have placed their power over us, because we understand now that they are part of God's wonderful creation, too — beautiful souls who have come in Unconditional Love. To work with us as we have worked with them. To bring forth the values from those life experiences that we have chosen, in a soap opera so gigantic and so complex that only the *Grand Master* could have written the script.

Affirmation to Reclaim My Power

From the Divine Love that flows through my Being:

I Love and Honor those

who have placed their power over me,

but I now choose

to return their power to them.

I now reclaim my birthright,

and I reclaim my Power,

and I will not relinquish it again.

So be it!

✧ ✧ ✧ ✧ ✧

The Lesson of Life: Have you ever watched a play in which every actor is working in harmony together to bring the story into its fulfillment? Now look at your life and those around you, and see life from a higher perspective. As a big stage play that continues to unfold, everyone acting out their parts in concert. As a continuing saga that changes with each thought, directed by yourself. You are not the spectator; you are the Author. Knowing this, how would you choose to write the script for your life story?

***Chakra #4 – From Bottom of Rib Cage to Top of Shoulders (Loving
Self):*** The *Love* chakra includes the shoulders, arms, upper back,
ribs, heart, lungs and breast in both male and female.

You have heard the same reports that I have. Heart disease is the
number one killer in our society today. Eighty-five percent will experience heart disease and more than fifty percent are actually dying from it.

You may also have heard that many young women today feel
they must compete for a career. The message some are sending to
their General (the subconscious), who has no sense of humor, is "if
I'm going to compete in this macho world and be successful, I must
become more like *them.*"

The General turns around and says, "Well, guys, if she needs to
become more like men, maybe she doesn't need *these.*"

One day she may wake up to find that she has a tumor in her
breast, and she will say, "My God, what did I ever do to deserve this?"

There is a beautiful lady that I have known for many years. She
grew up in that age we know as the Victorian Age, when men had all
the privileges and women had none. She was heard to repeat again
and again, "I wish I'd been born a man." Thus it was no surprise
that at a very young age she had a double mastectomy. We do
indeed create our own realities. Be careful of the words you choose.

All of our lives we have been told that it is selfish and self-centered
of us to think of ourselves first: "You must think of *others* first." Some
have told us this because that is what *they* were told. Others have said
it because they know that's how the game of *power and control* is played:
"If I can keep you from loving yourself, I've got you."

There are many people in our society under the illusion that they
love God. If you told them they didn't love God, they would become
very upset. "Of *course* I love God! What do you mean, I don't love
God?" But you cannot acknowledge love for the Creator and deny
Its creation in the same breath. When you acknowledge the divinity
within, you will truly know what it is to love the Creator.

> *You cannot acknowledge Love for the Creator*
> *and deny Its Creation in the same breath.*

Affirmation of Self-Worth

From the Divine Love that flows through my Being:

I declare my values,

my worth.

I am worthy of being Loved

and of Loving others.

Because what you see

is what you get.

So be it!

Although "what you see is what you get" has a note of humor, it also carries a very serious message. It says, "Don't ask me to change into something that you expect me to be, but love me for who I am, and I shall love you for who you are." It's called Unconditional Love.

✧ ✧ ✧ ✧ ✧

Chakra #5 – From Top of Shoulders to Bridge of Nose (Communication with Being): The neck, thyroid, mouth, lips, sinus, nose, etc. It is with the lips that we verbally acknowledge the divinity within.

Chakra #6 – The Eyes and Ears (Seeing and Hearing God in All Things).

Chakra #7 – Top of Head (The Divinity Within).

Affirmation for the Three Higher Chakras

From the Divine Love that flows through my Being:

With these lips, I speak God in all things;

with these ears, I hear God in all things;

and with these eyes, I see God in all things.

I now command my Crown Chakra to be open

and bring forth to me those Laws I have owned

through all Time and Space and Beyond

that have created these Judgments

that have not brought me Joy.

Bring them forth before me now

so that I may see them

and release them.

So be it!

✧　✧　✧　✧　✧

Desires of the Heart

You have now cleared the way to call forth the desires of your heart.

While I would like to say that the following affirmation is very powerful, I am aware that all affirmations are powerful. The following affirmation is the one that I personally focused on when my lungs became healed from asbestos poisoning.

Affirmation for the Desires of My Heart

From the Divine Love that flows through my Being:

I open my Mind, Body and Soul

and ask that you fill my Being

with your infinite Love,

your infinite Healing,

your infinite Protection,

your infinite Power and Wisdom.

I now call forth my Grand Adventure,

in Feelings and Emotions,

in all things that come in Light and Love

that will bring me Happiness and Joy.

So be it!

✧ ✧ ✧ ✧ ✧

You may choose to add any specific affirmations you feel are appropriate at this time. If either of the following two affirmations meet your desires, you may choose to use them.

Affirmation to Call Forth My Prosperity

From the Divine Love that flows through my Being:

I call forth my Abundance and Prosperity

in all forms that will bring me Happiness and Joy.

So be it!

✧ ✧ ✧ ✧ ✧

I asked a client if she desired to call forth someone to share her life with. Her response was, "I've been beat up enough." Many are calling forth someone to share their life, but have given no qualifications. *You get what you ask for.* I then offered her the following affirmation and she accepted it.

Affirmation to Call Forth a Sharer

From the Divine Love that flows through my Being:

I call forth a Sharer,

One who is my equal,

who will grow as I grow,

that we may grow together.

So be it!

✧ ✧ ✧ ✧ ✧

The mind has been in control for a long time. Now we are being told to get in touch with our intuitive feelings.

Affirmation to the Mind

From the Divine Love that flows through my Being:

I give my Mind permission

to give me Reason and Logic,

but I do not give it permission

to tell me what to do.

So be it!

✦ ✦ ✦ ✦ ✦

Have you heard about those old tapes that keep playing over again and again in our minds? You may decide to change direction in your life, but often old messages keep drawing you back into old patterns.

Affirmation to Release Control Patterns

From the Divine Love that flows through my Being:

whatever Laws that I have owned

regarding my control patterns,

through all Time and Space and Beyond

and on all levels of my Being,

I now choose to release.

So be it!

✦ ✦ ✦ ✦ ✦

Since thought is the most powerful energy in the universe, it is essential that your thoughts resonate at the highest vibration of Universal Love.

Affirmation to Transmute Thought Forms and Thought Patterns

From the Divine Love that flows through my Being:

I call forth all my Thought Forms and Thought Patterns –

through all Time and Space and Beyond

and on all levels of my Being –

to stand before me now

as I stand before you – in Love.

I now choose to transmute

my Thought Forms and Thought Patterns

into Unconditional Love.

I now call forth only those Thought Forms and Thought Patterns

that will bring me Joy.

So be it!

Looking into our aura, we might also discover miscellaneous shadows, little fears that have come from a variety of sources. It is not important to focus on what caused them, but rather to choose to transmute them to Unconditional Love.

Affirmation to Transmute the Shadows of My Being

From the Divine Love that flows through my Being:

I call forth the Shadows of my Being –

on all levels of my Being,

through all Time and Space and Beyond –

to stand before me now

as I stand before you – in Love.

I thank you for the lessons we have shared,

but I now choose to transmute these Shadows

into Unconditional Love.

So be it!

✧   ✧   ✧   ✧   ✧

If we could see into our aura, we might find some voids, or empty spaces. Empty spaces have a way of filling up quickly with something. We choose to fill those spaces with Unconditional Love.

Affirmation to Fill My Being with Love

I now command that all Voids of my Being –

through all Time and Space and Beyond

and on all levels of my Being –

now be filled with Unconditional Love.

So be it!

✧   ✧   ✧   ✧   ✧

Addictions take many forms: alcohol, smoking, chocolate, eating, drugs (including prescription drugs), as well as addictions to emotional disturbances such as despair and worry. I do not consider any of these wrong. However, if it is something that begins to control you, it is an addiction and now interferes with your free-will choice.

Worrying is simply meditating on the negative.

Affirmation to Release Addictions

From the Divine Love that flows through my Being:
I call forth my Addictions to stand before me now.
I thank you for the lessons that we have shared,
but I now choose to release all bonds between us
except for those of Unconditional Love.
I release these addictions to the Light.
I choose to reclaim my Power,
and I will not relinquish it again.
So be it!

✧　✧　✧　✧　✧

Have you ever set boundaries? Most of us have, at one time or another either consciously or at another level of consciousness. A boundary is a wall that we build so that no one can encroach upon us. It is also a wall that we cannot grow beyond. Now that we are aware of the totality of our Being, it is desirable that we grow without limitations. The following affirmation allows us to exchange those boundaries for free-will choice.

Affirmation to Release Boundaries and Limitations

From the Divine Love that flows through my Being:

All Laws that I have owned

regarding my boundaries and limitations –

through all Time and Space and Beyond –

and on all levels of my Being –

I release.

I declare that I have no boundaries and limitations,

and I give myself permission to be all that I AM,

to stand in my Truth

in Unconditional Love,

with no judgment of myself

or of others.

I honor all others for the journey they have chosen,

but I now choose to be the observer

and not a participator,

if that is what I choose in the moment.

So be it!

✧   ✧   ✧   ✧   ✧

Over time, each person has created many bonds. The bonds that we are addressing at this time are those that would interfere with our free-will choice. Our words, our thoughts and our actions have literally created shackles of energy that prevent us from moving ahead in life. We will also call forth the elementals, the consciousness that is attached to other forms of energy. Have you ever cursed the darkness or resented the rain? The vibration of every thought is recorded and cataloged in our consciousness and in our universe.

It is time to release them and prepare for a more important journey. I invite you to join me now in a beautiful visualization, as we prepare for this aspect of the Healing.

Walk with me, if you will, down a beautiful pathway. The fragrance of the flowers that line the way fill your senses. A continuous wall of crystals has formed on both sides, creating an energy that enhances your radiance.

As you move along the path, you become aware that with each step your worries, your fears and judgments are diminishing. All negativity within every cell of your body and every vibration of your Being is being released and transmuted by the crystals into the purest vibration of Unconditional Love. You feel your entire Being become lighter with each movement.

Radiating in the pure vibration of love, you come to the end of the path at the top of the hill. You are standing before a stairway leading to a Sacred Temple. I can go no farther with you, for this is your temple. It is one that you have built with your own thoughts, using materials of your choice that bring you great joy.

Ascending the stairs, you enter your temple. The feeling of Unconditional Love that is present is beyond anything you have ever experienced. It is here that you may call forth and embrace the Creator God, the Creator of all things. It is here, within this beautiful temple, that we will choose to release all bonds that have not brought us joy.

Affirmation to Release Bonds

From the Divine Love that flows through my Being:

All Souls, Elementals and Thought Forms that I call forth this day,

it is my intent that all aspects of their Souls

and all aspects of my Soul be present,

and that this reflect, through all Time and Space and Beyond

and on all levels of our Being.

I call forth the Nucleus of our Beings,

the Core of our Wholeness,

to participate in this Healing.

Call each person forth that you feel has played an important role in your life. That role may have brought you joy or pain. I offer a suggested list: grandparents, parents, brothers/sisters, spouse and/or former spouses, children and unborn children. Relationships, both personal and business.

Any other specific person or group of persons who have created drama in your life.

Repeat the affirmation that follows as often as necessary until you have addressed all who have played key roles in your life. Do not cut this process short. And do not underestimate the importance of this as it relates to the Healing.

From the Divine Love that flows through my Being:
I now call forth [name] to stand before me
as I stand before you – in Love.
I ask now that you forgive me as I forgive you.
I embrace you in Love
and I thank you for the lessons that we have shared,
but I now choose to release to the Light
all bonds between us except those of Unconditional Love.
I bid you to go in Peace.
So be it!

Once you have called those forth by name, conclude with the following.

From the Divine Love that flows through my Being:
I now call forth all Souls, Elementals and Thought Forms
to stand before me as I stand before you – in Love.
I ask now that you forgive me as I forgive you.
I embrace you in Love
and I thank you for the lessons that we have shared,
but I now choose to release to the Light
all bonds between us except those of Unconditional Love.
I bid you to go in Peace.
So be it!

After completing the above, add the following affirmation.

I release to the Light at this time
absolutely everything that is not of the Light,
on any dimension,
within any part of my Body, my Mind and my Soul,
within the Nucleus of my Being.
I am at one with God at this time.
So be it!

✧　✧　✧　✧　✧

The remaining affirmations are self-explanatory.

Affirmation to Remember My Creativity and Divinity

From the Divine Love that flows through my Being:
I call forth my Angels to stand before me now
as I stand before you – in Love.
I ask you now to assist me in remembering
my Creativity and my Divinity.
I ask that you bring this forth
in a manner that will bring Joy to my heart
and a smile to my lips.
I look forward to your presence always.
So be it!

✧　✧　✧　✧　✧

Affirmation Aligning the Being in Perfection

From the Divine Love that flows through my Being:

In the name of the Creator

and from the Divine Love that flows through my Being,

I command that every cell in my body

and every vibration of my Being

align itself in Divine Perfection,

for I desire to be all that I AM.

I choose to be all that I AM.

I AM all that I AM.

And I now call forth my Identity in Divine Perfection.

So be it!

✧ ✧ ✧ ✧ ✧

Affirmation to Acknowledge My Creation

From the Divine Love that flows through my Being:
I call forth every cell in my body
and every vibration of my Being
to stand before me now,
as I stand before you – in Love.
I acknowledge my Love for you.
I acknowledge the hard work that you have performed for me
to support me in my journey.
And I now choose, and I ask of you
that you align yourself with the Nucleus of my Being
in Divine Perfection and according to my Heart's Desire,
and to integrate with me once again in Mind, Body and Soul
as I move forward now in my journey.
So be it!

✧   ✧   ✧   ✧   ✧

Patience is not waiting three hours in a dentist's office for a tooth to be drilled. *Patience is the time between when you ask for a Healing and when it fully manifests according to your desires.* If you weighed 300 pounds and you desired to weigh 150 pounds, it would be inappropriate to lose that much weight instantly. It would create so much stress on the physical body that it could be fatal. Healing occurs in God's time, not ours. Allow the Divinity Within to manifest in a manner that will be loving and nurturing to you.

Allowing means just that. If you are expecting, looking, hoping, you are not allowing. You are interfering with the Divine process. Although some Healings can take place almost instantly, you will more often find that it is gradual. The body must now decide how it wants to release all of that baggage it has been carrying.

I once assisted a ninety-year-old woman who had lost the sight of one eye. Midway through the Healing her sight totally returned. However, recovery for most people has been gradual, and a few have noticed little or no change. As the facilitator, I am not in charge — the people who receive the Healing are. Are they *really* prepared to accept a Healing at all levels of their Being?

The emotional cause affecting the loss of eyesight is the unwillingness to see something in their life. Not everyone is prepared to see or face their truths, even though they may emphatically believe so at the conscious level. Healing follows the total surrender to the desire to be well, whole and perfect in mind, body and soul. Be patient and allow the universe to manifest your desires.

"If ye believe and doubt not, nothing shall be impossible to you."

✧　✧　✧　✧　✧

To establish new thought patterns, repeat the following affirmation each day for the next twenty-one days.

Affirmation for Establishing New Patterns

From the Divine Love that flows through my Being

and the Nucleus of all that I AM:

I reaffirm the affirmations supporting my choice

to be Well, Whole and Perfect

in Mind, Body and Soul.

So be it!

✧　✧　✧　✧　✧

Clearing Your Relationships

If you are in a relationship (either personal, family or business) the distorted energies of another person can interfere with your relationship. You may choose to clear those interfering energies by asking those people: *"If there is anything interfering with our relationship, may I say a prayer to clear it?"*

If you receive their permission, you may go into your quiet space and silently (or aloud) say the following affirmation for them on their behalf.

Affirmations to Clear Relationship Entities

I now call forth [name] to stand before me,
as I stand before you – in Love.
On your behalf
I offer you this prayer to accept or reject
according to your Free-Will Choice.

From the Divine Love that flows through my Being:
Whatever laws I have owned,
whatever beliefs I may hold,
whatever vows I have made,
whatever contracts or agreements I have made
and those I have made them with –
through all Time and Space and Beyond
and on all levels of my Being –
that have created these judgments within my Being
that are not bringing me Happiness and Joy,
I now choose to release.
Goodby and God bless.

I now call forth the Angels of Divine Perfection
to assist me in restoring myself
and my property, past, present and future,
and the Elementals attached to that property,
all to its Divine Perfection.

I call forth the Shadow of Fear,

including all laws, judgments and fears relating to it,

as well as all property that I own, past, present and future,

to stand before me now, as I stand before you – in Love.

I ask you now to forgive me as I forgive you.

I thank you for the lessons that we have shared,

but I now choose to release all bonds between us

except for those of Unconditional Love.

I now choose to transmute

those laws, judgments, fears and property

into Unconditional Love.

I bid you to go in Peace.

So be it!

✧ ✧ ✧ ✧ ✧

Following a Healing, you will go through a process of detoxing. The body has been holding on to a lot of emotions, translated into physical form, which it now wants to release. For the next few days you may feel a need for extra rest and self-nurture as this change takes place. It is part of the Healing process.

Be kind to yourself. I suggest that you treat yourself to a hot Epsom salts bath. Use 3 or 4 handfuls of Epsom salts in a bathtub of warm water (as warm as possible, but still comfortable), adding hot water as needed. This will open the pores and help draw out the toxins, assisting in the detoxing process. Remain in the tub for about thirty minutes. Relax, play some music, make it a pleasant experience. Sleep well.

Disease cannot exist in a cell where the love of God is present.

Freedom

The greatest freedom of all
is to be free of fear
to know life as an adventure
in constant motion
in harmony with the rhythm of the Universe

Bringing forth the desires of the heart
as life unfolds through creative manifestation
with no stagnation from judgment
fear or worry

To know the gentle strength of Unconditional Love
being able to see the perfection in all things
to live a life of trust
without worry

Like a child watching a magic show
in anticipation of the next event
totally open to receive
the joy of all possibilities

The Frog Story

It is true that if you place a frog into a pan of hot water, it will jump out almost before it hits the water. However, if you place the same frog into a pan of cold water and very slowly raise the temperature, it will never think to jump until it is too late.

The human life form is much the same. It has been demonstrated many times. Over the years we accumulate layers of distorted energy patterns through our judgments and fears. Then one day we discover disease and disharmony in our emotional or physical body and wonder where it came from. Many never jump until it is too late.

The Lessons I Have Been Taught

Life is a lesson.

Life is a series of lessons.

It is for these lessons that we have come here.

Here on Earth.

The lessons?

To experience our feelings and emotions.

And so it has been with me.

Each year, each day, each moment, brings another experience. But it is the last four months of my daughter's life that I refer to in this writing. My daughter Lisa. She is twenty-five years old.

It was early October when Lisa asked if she might move in with me until she could find employment and get on her feet financially. She had not been employed since early August. Unknown to me, she had not been feeling well, but thought that things would improve soon. During that time I had been traveling extensively for my company and I was only home for a day or so before going out for another week or two.

Upon returning home from a trip in early November, I noticed that Lisa's skin and eyes were quite yellow. I realized that she had jaundice, a condition resulting from a liver dysfunction where toxins were backing up in her system. She made an appointment to see a doctor, and after an examination and a blood test it was suspected that she had hepatitis. The test results came back the following Monday. She was told that a doctor had been alerted to receive her immediately at the hospital's emergency room.

She was admitted and the tests began. During her examination, they found a ruptured tumor in the uterus that was bleeding uncontrollably, so blood transfusions were immediately begun. Suspecting cancer, they would need biopsies to confirm it. Thus numerous tests were ordered, including a CAT scan, x-rays and a laparoscopy. A laparoscopy involves an incision near the navel, where a tube is inserted that permits blowing the patient up with carbon dioxide gas, much like a balloon. Then a second tube is inserted that has optics to probe the abdominal area. In Lisa's case, they decided to make three additional incisions across the abdomen for a more intensive exploration — a total of four incisions in a patient who was already bleeding uncontrollably! Over the next few days they would take nine biopsies, each causing another area of bleeding that also required healing.

The tests confirmed that the liver and kidneys were enlarged. The swelling had caused enough pressure to close off the ducts (or passageways), preventing the liver from draining the toxins. They inserted a shunt (a small tube) via the mouth down through the body and into the area of blockage. This procedure successfully opened the passageway and allowed the toxins to drain. She improved quite noticeably in two or three days, and her condition continued to improve. The kidneys, however, started to fail, and continued to deteriorate over the following weeks.

The real concern at this time was the suspected cancer. We awaited the lab reports, which took several days to arrive. In the meantime, the team of doctors were becoming frustrated as the bleeding continued: a total of sixteen pints of blood were administered in nine days.

In spite of extreme pressure from the doctors, Lisa steadfastly refused chemotherapy, for which I commended her. The doctors did not know of any way to stop the bleeding and hoped that chemotherapy would shrink the tumors, allowing the bleeding to stop.

Biopsies confirmed their suspicion that lymphoma tumors and tissue had compromised the liver, kidneys, pancreas, stomach, uterus, and ovaries. There was extensive mestastasis throughout the abdominal area. The doctor assured us that the medical journals showed a 50% cure rate (using the recommended chemotherapy) for this type of cancer. We were later told separately by other doctors on staff that there was, variously, a 60%, a 65% and a 95%

cure rate, also quoted from the *same* medical journals. We asked for this in writing, but they would not comply with our request. They would soon find that we were quite knowledgeable in the area of cancer.

Lisa was informed that she had an advanced case and they would need to use a "big hammer" (heavy chemotherapy), which would cause her to lose her hair and probably become sterile. What the doctors did not know is that I too have studied the medical journals, which indicate there is possibly a 50% chance of remission *if the cancer is confined to a single location.* However, when the cancer has metastasized to two or more areas, there is little that modern medicine can do. In fact, medical studies have shown that those people *not* receiving chemotherapy and radiation actually live longer than those who do.

Lisa was well aware of the toxic side effects of chemotherapy.

> Dr. Samuel Epstein, from the University of Illinois College of Medicine, testifying before the 100th Congress of the United States in his report on cancer, stated, "Apart from the immediate toxicity, such treatment as chemotherapy and radiation, while effective, can increase the subsequent risk of developing a secondary cancer by up to 100 times."

Of most concern at this time was the uncontrolled bleeding from the uterus. On the evening of the ninth day, I asked the doctor in charge of the case what method would be the most effective in controlling the bleeding. He answered, "Tying off the two arteries that feed the uterus."

I asked why he had not done this.

He replied, "Because the vaginal wall is compromised with malignant tissue."

At that time I received a psychic message, "Perhaps you can't, but we can."

Most people today understand what visualization is. With your

eyes closed, you visualize what you want to achieve. Many professional athletes do this while sitting in a chair before the game.
Golfers may see themselves practicing their golf swing, seeing and
feeling every motion throughout the swing, making each move in
perfection, sinking putt after putt. If you visualize yourself getting
well – your disease healing, the bleeding stopping – this is in reality
spiritual healing, since only energy is being used, and energy is
spiritual, not physical by our definition. Yes, even professional athletes work with spiritual energy, and most likely you have, too.
Incidentally, positive thinking is also spiritual.

If you visualize *yourself* getting well, this is called visualization.
However, if I visualize Lisa getting well (with her permission), then it
is called etheric healing, psychic healing, spiritual healing, laying-on
of hands. Call it what you will, it is all the same thing.

As soon as the doctor left the room, I turned to Lisa and asked,
"Is it your desire to have the bleeding stopped?"

"Oh, yes," she replied.

"Then with your permission, may I assist you?"

She responded, "Yes, but please don't touch me. I'm in a great
deal of pain from all the surgery."

"That will not be necessary," I replied. I then held my hands a
few inches above her lower abdomen, closed my eyes and visualized
my fingers sliding under the artery, pulling a waxed cord around the
artery and firmly tying it tight. I repeated the same thing on the
second artery. I visualized the bleeding coming to a trickle and then
stopping. At this time the bleeding stopped, and there was no more
bleeding from this location in the remaining weeks.

The next morning I asked the oncologist, "How is the bleeding?"

He looked at the nurse who was present and asked her the same
question. She replied, "We haven't had to use any more pads since
last night" (pads to absorb the blood).

I looked at Lisa and winked. She smiled and winked back.

In the hallway I met the doctor in charge of the case and again
asked about the bleeding. He stated, "I never look at what's coming
out (blood), but rather what's going in, and there have been no more

transfusions since last night."

Lisa has always been very spiritually aware. She knew as well as I that neither the doctor nor I can heal anyone, and that in fact patients heal themselves. The doctor or the facilitator can only provide the tools for patients to use in healing themselves. Healing cannot occur without the patient's permission at some level of consciousness. Lisa's faith had proven this to be correct.

It was at this time that I received a psychic message: *"Lisa will be healed, and in a time not too distant she will be able to take care of herself."*

On the twelfth day the doctors said to Lisa, "Since the bleeding has stabilized and the liver has been draining well, and since you refuse to accept our recommendation for chemotherapy, you may as well check yourself out and pursue whatever treatment you choose. However, the kidneys are not functioning well and will only get worse."

Lisa signed herself out and went home.

The hospital stay had not been a pleasant one for Lisa. When she entered the hospital, she felt a bit punk as a result of the toxins that were in her system and, of course, she was a bit concerned.

During her stay she had received very poor nutrition. The first few days were full of medical tests that required her to abstain from food and, in some cases, liquids. For long periods she had no food other than IV fluids. On the morning of the fifth day in the hospital Lisa told me she had not had anything to eat for some time. They'd scheduled a CAT-scan that morning and she was to get breakfast afterwards. Later they informed her that they were running behind schedule, that the scan would not be until that night, so she couldn't have anything to eat until the next day. When I returned that afternoon, I found they had given her barium for an upper and lower GI test they planned the next morning, which meant she would not be receiving any food until even later.

I called the nurse in and said, "Nurse, I have been around the medical profession long enough to be qualified to make this statement. It's unfortunate that sometimes doctors get so wrapped up in medical technology that they forget the needs of the patient. This young lady is badly in need of rest and nutrition and she has had neither since she has been here. Are you going to give her dinner tonight?"

"I don't know," she replied. "I will do what the doctor tells me to do."

She returned a few minutes later with a tray of food.

With all the tests that were taking place, it is understandable that Lisa was kept busy with doctors and nurses running in and out of her room, poking her (even when she was sleeping at night), taking blood samples and other endless medical activities. This continued every few minutes, day and night. With the added stress of fasting, she was completely exhausted. It was difficult, if not impossible, to sleep in the daytime, as there was construction on the floor below. The loud noise of jackhammers could not only be heard, but the vibration could be felt through the floor all the way up her bedframe. Her spirits had remained high and her attitude positive, but at this point she broke down and cried. I held her hand and said, "Lisa, you are in charge."

She replied, "I don't feel that I'm in charge."

I said, "People can steal your power only if you allow them to."

The next time the doctor and nurse came barging into the room unannounced, Lisa stated in no uncertain terms that this was *her* room and she demanded her privacy. Her door was to remain closed, and anyone who wished to come in could knock. If she felt up to it, she would ask them in. If she was asleep and did not respond, they were to stay out and come back later. This would apply not only to them, but to her mother, father, brother and friends. Lisa took her *power* back and never gave it up again. I was proud of her. We respected her wishes; we knocked first.

When she left the hospital, she was unable to sit up or roll over by herself due to the four incisions and nine biopsies, which caused her considerable discomfort. This was also complicated by the severe abdominal pain resulting from the carbon dioxide still in her abdomen. (If you have ever had severe stomach cramps due to trapped gas, multiply this many times and you can appreciate the problem. Nurses tell me that if doctors ever had a laparoscopy, they would never prescribe one again.) Furthermore, Lisa was severely chafed between her legs due to the continual wet pads. As if this were not enough, she had retained more than 25 pounds of water, mostly from the waist down, as a result of the fluids given through IVs. Her legs and ankles were swollen to the point that the skin looked like it would burst. This left her unable to walk without assistance, and then only with great difficulty.

There was a further complication that they never warn you about. Having a number of friends in the health field, we had been told to be alert for side effects caused from the blood transfusions.

I asked, "What effects?"

They answered, "Tell me who the blood donors were. Did the blood come from a male? A female? A night watchman? A pregnant woman? A drug addict? Lisa no longer has any of her own blood and is now compromised with any problems the donors had. One of those effects will most likely be itching until she starts making a blood supply of her own."

Lisa's itching was intense and became worse toward the early morning hours, when she wanted to literally tear the flesh off her legs. In a few days, working with massage therapy, acupressure, spiritual healing and simple techniques, we were successful in removing the twenty-five pounds of water she had gained from the IVs. The stomach pains were all but gone as well as pain from the thirteen surgical incisions, and she was able to get up and move around under her own power. The daily improvement was encouraging.

Two days before Thanksgiving Lisa threw up a large volume of blood along with fibrous material from the tumor that had caused the stomach blockage and made it difficult for her to hold food down. We saw this as a positive sign, that the body was eliminating something that didn't belong there.

The following night (Thanksgiving eve) Lisa again threw up a large amount of blood. But this time she arose to go to the bathroom, became faint and momentarily went into shock. I immediately called 911, and shortly thereafter she was readmitted into emergency at the hospital. Blood transfusions were ordered. Her stomach was flushed out and a scope inserted in an effort to find out what caused the bleeding. We were informed that there were two or more sites near where the stomach meets the small intestine that were seeping blood, and since it was a lymphoma site, they could not cauterize it. Again, there was nothing they could do but continue transfusions.

I said to myself, You can't, but *we* can. Immediately the word "fusion" entered my thoughts, and I knew that was what I had to do. As soon as the doctor left, I turned to Lisa. "Is it your desire to have this bleeding stopped?" I asked.

"Yes," she responded.

"May I assist you?"

Again her response was affirmative.

I closed my eyes, held my hands above the area involved and visualized light beaming like a laser onto the affected site. In my mind's eye I saw a scab forming over the area and the bleeding stop. They would give her two pints of blood, but there was no further loss of blood following the healing. Forty-eight hours after her admission, she was again released to go home.

Again we worked at removing several pounds of water that she retained after only two days in the hospital. Things went fairly well for several weeks. Her spirits were always high and her attitude was positive. Being very sensitive to energy, she could sense those persons with positive or negative attitudes. Those who were positive were welcome. Those with negative thoughts were not. She had enough to contend with without having to support someone else and their problems.

Lisa's kidneys had continued to deteriorate and examinations indicated kidney failure. Dialysis was scheduled.

Once again Lisa's condition deteriorated. Her blood pressure had dropped dramatically, and for the third time I called 911. She was stabilized with fluids, was made quite comfortable and had several good days.

Thursday, January 30, she sat up in a recliner most of the day and ate well. When I arrived after work, I asked Lisa, "What would you like to do?"

Lisa said, "I want to talk to you."

"That's fine," I said. "What would you like to talk about?"

She made herself comfortable and looked at me. "Dad, I realize that if I am to continue my life, I must assume certain responsibilities, and I don't know if I can handle that."

I responded, "Lisa, not only can you do it, you will be great at it."

She looked me with piercing eyes and said with conviction, "Dad, don't lecture me. *Listen* to me!"

Her words rang in my ears. She was trying to tell me something and I was not listening. I am very much aware that a good communicator is first, and most importantly, a good listener. I had not been a good communicator. She was desperately trying to tell me something of major importance that was happening in her life. Something that would determine whether she would remain here or go on to other things. I listened. After all, it made little difference what *I* wanted for Lisa (or the doctor or anyone else, for that matter), but what Lisa wanted for Lisa.

We had a nice visit that evening and she was quite content. At 11:00 p.m., she threw up a large quantity of fluid, largely blood, and the nurse read her blood pressure at 50/30. Several attendants immediately began to take her, bed and all, to intensive care. Lisa insisted on getting into a wheelchair, but they assured her that at this time she might become dizzy and pass out. They called for two more units of blood and injected a drug intended to stabilize the blood pressure. I was called to the phone just outside of her room, where I had a clear view of what was going on inside. I counted eleven doctors, nurses and attendants trying everything they knew to keep Lisa alive.

Her situation was critical.

It was 11:30 p.m. and the doctor was talking to me on the phone. "Mr. Work, what do I do if Lisa stops breathing in fifteen minutes?"

For the first time I felt the urgency of the situation. I replied, "I want you to do what is necessary to keep her alive." The psychic message that had come to me was always ringing in my ears. *Lisa will be healed, and in a time not too distant, she will be able to take care of herself.* I had never visualized Lisa other than getting well.

The doctor continued. "Mr. Work, your daughter is terminal. It would be a terrible thing to put her on life-support systems, forcing her to breathe. We are giving her medication intended to stabilize her blood pressure. In a critical case, we give twenty units. Mr. Work, we are giving Lisa seventy-five units, and she is still not responding. What do you want me to do?"

I stated, "You may consider her terminal, but we believe in a higher Source."

"I understand," he said, "but medicine is limited in what it can do."

I replied, "Continue to support her as you have, with blood, oxygen, IV fluids and any medication for pain. Should she stop breathing, make one honest attempt at CPR. If she does not respond, then nothing else should be done."

I returned to Lisa's bedside. It would be another hour before they received the blood they had asked for. She had a transparent oxygen mask on. I placed my hands on her hand and shoulder and began my healing prayers. With my eyes closed, I could see a fog. I said silently, "Lisa, let me help you across the threshold." I could see the fog starting to part, and then suddenly I realized I was looking at her soul. I exclaimed aloud, "My God, I'm looking at your soul!"

Lisa had been drifting between dimensions, and I was aware that she had been talking aloud to her spiritual guides and Angels, laughing and carrying on a lively conversation. I thought I heard her saying (rather garbled behind the oxygen mask), "Talk to me, talk to me, talk to me."

I thought she was still talking to her guides, but suddenly I realized she might be talking to me. I responded, "Lisa, I love you," and began saying my healing prayers aloud. Immediately she relaxed and breathed peacefully. Since the time she had entered the room, her eyes had been closed.

Within the hour, before they received the blood for her, she was sitting up in bed, quite relaxed, comfortable, totally aware, her blood pressure normal. She looked at me, and to the best of her ability tried to explain what had happened. She held her hands up to one side and said, "Dad, over here I could see everything that has happened in my life, and I knew why I am the way I am." Then moving her hands to the other side, she said, "Then I could see everything very clearly, and I knew what I had to do to change everything." Looking directly at me with an angelic look on her face and speaking with wisdom coming from her soul, she said, "Dad, everything is going to be all right!"

I mentioned that she had been saying, "Talk to me, talk to me."

She laughed. "Yes, I remember that. I kept asking you to talk to me, and when no one answered, I thought I was dead."

We laughed.

I pulled a reclining chair next to her bed. The nurse gave me a blanket. I placed my hand in Lisa's and I remained with her throughout the night. And every night from then on.

Her blood pressure was normal and other vital signs were stable. When she was admitted to intensive care, they inserted a tube through the nostril and into the stomach so that it would continually drain fluids and blood into a clear container mounted on the wall above her head. Previously, internal bleeding would make its way into the stomach, and after enough had collected, it would cause her to feel nauseous and finally throw it up, leaving her drained of energy. The tube would prevent this and conserve her energy.

Saturday she received dialysis, and I returned to find that she had been given another three units of blood. This made a total of thirty-three.

That day a friend and I were in the room with Lisa, one on each side of the bed. She gave a smile of satisfaction and said, "I'm so happy the two of you are here." We acknowledged that we felt the same, and each of us took one of her hands between ours and held them for nearly an hour. We could feel the energy flow through us to her, and from her to us. She would look from one, then to the other. Much of the time she was looking over our heads and around our bodies. She had the strangest look, one of awe, and we knew that she was looking at our auras. Each passing day she was drifting more and more between dimensions, between physical and spiritual awareness. Lisa was very peaceful. It was a beautiful experience.

At one point Lisa looked intently at her fingers. After a time she said, "Dad, I could see it [energy] coming out here," pointing at her fingertip, "and going in here," pointing at another fingertip. Then looking directly at me, with an angelic look about her, she said, "Everything is going to be fine."

On Sunday Lisa's friends dropped by one by one. She was delighted and quite alert the entire time. After they left, I returned to be with Lisa. It was 8:00 p.m.

I noticed that her blood pressure was dropping. She was picking at the tape on her nose that for the past three days had held the stomach tube in place. It was annoying and caused her a great deal of discomfort.

By 10:00 p.m.Lisa was drifting between dimensions. She was in a state of consciousness where she could be talking to me and then be in another world communicating telepathically (or speaking out loud) with her spiritual guides.

Suddenly she grasped the tube coming from her nose with both hands and began to pull it out. I grabbed her hands and shouted, "Lisa, stop that!"

Immediately, two nurses came running in and grabbed one hand and I the other. The three of us could not stop her, as she screamed, "Take it out! Take it out!"

She had already removed it about six inches. I looked at the nurse and said, "Nurse, please take the tube out." Lisa had not been passing any blood from the stomach for some time. Again I repeated, "Please take the tube out. It's okay. We can always put it in later if we feel it's necessary."

The nurse then withdrew the tube, and Lisa looked at the nurse calmly and in a soft voice said simply, "Thank you."

She had reclaimed her power. She was in charge. She knew exactly what she was doing. She was preparing for a greater journey, and she didn't want to go with a tube sticking out of her nose. She was noticeably more comfortable and at peace.

A few minutes later she looked up and to the right side of her bed. I had been standing to the left the entire time. As she looked up, her mouth dropped open in awe. Looking back and forth across a section to the right of her bed, with an expression of total amazement on her face, she said, "Where...where did you all come from?"

She looked and listened intently. Then, after a brief pause, a look of pure ecstasy came over her as she exclaimed excitedly, "Yes! Oh, yes! Oh, yes! Oh, yes!" I knew that her guides had just asked her if she was ready to go home.

Only moments afterward, she turned to me, with excitement still in her voice and said, "Dad, you don't know, do you? You just don't know."

I answered, "Lisa, there are many things I don't know. Would you tell me about it?" She thought for a moment, then replied, "Dad, I don't know how." Then tenderly she said, "I love you."

A few minutes later she sat forward in bed, looking to her left toward the foot of the bed. Her face lit up with an expression of pure delight, as if she had just witnessed a great magical act, and said excitedly, "Wow! That's pretty *#?# good!" Whatever she had seen had brought her pure joy.

I was very much aware that her eyes had changed this evening. I mean, they had physically changed. The entire eye was larger. Not only the pupil, but the entire colored area of the eye. Looking into her pupils was like looking into a bottomless pool. I had read of this occurring to those who are about to cross over into spirit, but this was the first time I had personally experienced it. I recognized that this physical change in the eyes permits us to see in a different dimension. She had spent much of the evening looking around my head at my aura. It was evident that as the minutes wore on, she was moving closer to her true spiritual form.

Her pulse rate had been running at 150 per minute ever since I had come into the room, and her breathing was labored, much like an asthmatic who struggles to take in a deep breath. But now it was becoming more noticeable.

Only a few minutes since her last delightful statement, she turned to look me directly in the eye, and said very seriously, "Dad, if I can answer the question, why won't you let me die?"

I replied, "Lisa, I am not holding you back. Is that your desire?"

"Yes," she answered, "I want to die, I want to die." Her statement was not one of a person who had a death wish as we know it, but rather of one who realized that if she were to go on in her spiritual journey, that is the doorway that one goes through.

I added, "Lisa, I love and honor you. I am here only to help you through your journey, wherever that may take you." I leaned over her, gave her a gentle hug, and whispered in her ear, "I love you."

She whispered back, "I love you too, Daddy."

Her breathing was quite heavy for a few seconds as she looked deeply into my eyes. Her pulse rate on the monitor began to slow to 120 beats. She closed her eyes and her breathing eased. Then she took two long and relaxed breaths, as if she were falling asleep.

It was 11:00 p.m.

And she was gone.

I pressed the call button and the nurse responded immediately. I suspect she had been watching her monitor at her desk. I said, "Nurse, CPR, *NOW!*"

She entered the room quickly as other attendants responded to the call. The nurse suggested that I would be more comfortable in the waiting room, and they would come and get me as soon as they had something to report. I complied.

A few minutes later, the nurse, accompanied by a lady physician, came into the waiting room. With an expression of serious concern for my own welfare, the doctor said, "Mr. Work, I'm sorry, but Lisa did not respond to CPR."

I reached out and placed my hand on her shoulder and replied in a gentle voice, "It's all right, doctor, it's all right. This is where Lisa's soul wants to be at this time."

I returned to the room and stood beside Lisa and held her hand. As I looked down at her, I said, "Lisa, where did I go wrong in my interpretation of the message I received?" *Lisa will be healed, and in a time not too distant, she will be able to take care of herself.*

No sooner had I asked the question than the answer hit me with its full impact. I had been looking through my physical eyes, not my spiritual eyes.

This was her Healing.

And she was "now able to care for herself."

How well I knew that for some, death as we know it is the Healing.

I had been hearing what I wanted to hear. I had been looking at life in a materialistic form, not seeing life as it really is, in the grand concept of the greater Divine Plan of which we are all a part.

Life as we know and think of it is the illusion in which we are participating for the moment. Our spiritual nature is the reality. Lisa was very much aware of that reality as her time came near. This is what she was trying to tell me when she said, "Dad, you don't know, do you? You just don't know."

Yes, I did know. But in the effort to see life as I wanted it to be, I had forgotten.

✧　✧　✧　✧　✧

As a parent, you raise your children to the best of your ability, acting as their guardian, protector and teacher. You share hardships, anger, frustrations, as well as those happy times. Memories that will last forever. And yes, love. But in the end it was Lisa who would become my teacher.

With lessons of faith, courage, patience, compassion and love.

Faith: This we shared from the beginning of her adventure. Faith that the healing we had asked for we would indeed receive. There were many healings along the way. Healings within Lisa. Healings within the family. Healings with her loved ones and friends.

Courage: Her spirits always remained high. Her positive attitude was unshakable. Never once did I hear her complain.

Compassion: Everything that had happened in our lives in previous years seemed to melt away with the reality of the moment. I no longer saw my little girl, but a young lady faced with tough decisions. A young lady who needed my help more than the little girl ever did. She was dependent on someone almost twenty-four hours a day: to buy food; to cook; to massage her swollen legs and feet and the back that hurt from too much lying in bed; to take her to the doctors, to dialysis, and yes, at times even to the bathroom.

Patience: Patience is a most misunderstood word. Patience has not to do with holding one's "temper" inside! Patience is true knowledge of, and true faith and trust in, the unfolding of Divine Order. Patience is the affirmation of the blessing while you are waiting for it to manifest. Patience is faith that the Divine Law of Love will unfold everything, manifest everything, provide everything. Patience is faith — learning that what we have sought in love, according to the laws, *WILL* be ours, *IS* ours and *IS MANIFEST* as the cycle of all unfolds. Learn to use your patience in the faith and knowledge that what you require will be given.

Love: Oh, yes. Love. How can I ever describe the feelings that had grown between us during these four months? A new respect. A new understanding. A new love for one another. Love: "A state of being without judgment." Unconditional Love.

Love, without judgment. To respect and support her decisions, decisions that only she can make. Decisions that are right for her as she sees them, not as we want her to see them. According to her needs, not ours. This was her journey. No one could live it for her, and she would not permit anyone to do so. Decisions not to take chemotherapy or radiation despite the tremendous pressure by medical authorities and well-wishing friends. She knew her body better than they did. She knew that, by their diagnosis, she was already terminal. She knew and trusted her feelings that she would receive her Healing, if not in body, surely in spirit. After all, the healing you ask for is always received at some level, and where better than the soul?

Lisa knew that death is the natural progression in the continuation of life.

Lisa allowed me to share her experience through her thoughts, through her feelings; to see through her eyes. She allowed me to see beyond our mortal world into the eternal part of our nature, our eternal spirit. No, not something that is waiting for us in some· obscure place, but rather our spiritual Being that is ever present in us. A soul is not something you have; it is what you *are*.

That night, in her presence, I could feel her energy and that of her spiritual guides. By sharing her journey with me, it was she who became the teacher, and I, the student.

Yes, "the lessons I have been taught."

Everyone admired Lisa's long, full, beautiful hair. And she, in her determination, had said, "If I am going to go, I'm going to go with my hair."

And she did.

❖   ❖   ❖   ❖   ❖

Let us picture in our minds a beautiful blue lagoon on a clear day. A fine sailing ship spreads her brilliant white canvas in a fresh morning breeze and sails out to the open sea. We watch her grow smaller and smaller as she nears the horizon. Finally, where the sea and sky meet she slips silently from sight and someone near you says, "There, she is gone." Gone where? Gone from sight, that is all. She is still as large in mast and hull, still just as able to bear her load. We can be sure that just as we are saying, "There, she is gone," another is saying, "There she comes!" Life is eternal and love is immortal. And death is only a horizon, and a horizon is nothing save the limit of our sight. As one door closes another opens. While we are mourning the loss of a friend or loved one, others are rejoicing to meet them again beyond the veil.

– Author Unknown

❖   ❖   ❖   ❖   ❖

When someone is born, you are not sad. Why would you be sad because one has graduated and gone back?

We experience sadness because the human experience includes emotions. Some feel sadness when their children leave for their first day of kindergarten; when they leave home; when a daughter gets married. Some experience sadness when a loved one leaves to go on a trip that may take them away for some time. I would suggest that we exchange that sadness for joy. Joy for the new and exciting experience our loved ones are moving into. They have completed one experience — one more chapter of their journey. It is graduation day.

Find Joy in your heart for the Joy they will receive

as they move into their new spiritual experience.

Reversing the Aging Process

More articles are appearing whose topic is reversing the aging process. Is it possible to stop the aging process, let alone reverse it? The answer is yes, it is possible. Some people are even doing it, and many more will soon follow. As with most things in life, the process is not as difficult as you might think, but it does require a commitment.

Old age is a disease of the mind. It is time to eliminate this disease.

Before it is possible to reverse the aging process, you must first change your belief system. Our whole life has been one of reinforcing an age-old belief system that we get older, not younger. That the body deteriorates, not regenerates. We reinforce it continually with the most powerful energy in the universe — our thoughts.

"Both my father and grandfather lived till age seventy. I guess I have ten more years to go."

"The mind is the first thing to go. I can't remember what the second is."

"I guess this is what you expect when you get to be my age."

"When I retire, I'm just going to sit back and do nothing."

"No one in my family ever lived past sixty-seven."

"This must be what it's like to get old."

"I just feel worse every day."

One person's favorite saying was, "Nothing improves with age." For him, nothing ever did.

Have you ever noticed how the conversations change as you move through life?

When you are young, you talk about girls/boys.

After you get married, the subject changes to the children.

Later it becomes the grandchildren.

About that time, for many, their thoughts are preoccupied with comparing their illnesses and operations.

"I had triple-bypass heart surgery!"

"That's nothing. I had a five-way bypass, a gall bladder and a tumor removed."

It is the one thing that they have in common, and it becomes the focal point of many conversations. They associate disease with getting old. They do not realize that it is a sign of blocked energy, and that it is the blocked energy that leads to deterioration.

> *"You attract to you that on which you focus."*
> —The Universal Law of Magnetic Attraction

The Process of Regeneration

1. **Surrender** to the complete Healing Within. Release all energies that would create and/or support stress in your life.

2. **Eliminate** thoughts that reinforce old belief systems.

3. **Create** new thought patterns that will reinforce that which you desire. There are 100 trillion cells anxiously waiting for you to tell them what to do.

Dear God, each day I do indeed

become younger and more alive

in mind, body and spirit than the day before.

Thank you, God.

4. **The thymus gland** is one of the major glands within your body. It might be said that the thymus gland is the gateway to your immune system. Medical science understands that a child has a large thymus gland, and that "as you grow older" the thymus shrinks in size.

Ann Marie and I have a different theory. We believe that you grow older *because* the thymus gland is deteriorating. If you could stop the degeneration, you would stop the aging process. So if you reverse the process and begin to regenerate the thymus gland, you will reverse the aging process.

Dr. C. Samuel West, in his book *The Golden Seven Plus One* writes:

A statement written in a letter by Elisa Buenaventura. She has worked with cell cultures for many years as part of her cancer research.

She has worked at Boston Medical School, Tufts Medical School and Southern Medical School, conducting research in biophysics, cell biology and biochemistry.

She says, "Any medical researcher who has worked with

tissue cultures knows that cells can be kept alive indefinitely, but you must keep the chemical balance in and around the cells and eliminate the waste products of metabolism." She believes cells are meant to be eternal. They should not die or degenerate if the environment is kept clean, nutritious and chemically balanced.

Reversing the aging process is not simply a matter of eating the right foods. Good nourishment can assist in maintaining a good level of energy for the physical body. How well that food is digested and utilized by the body is directly related to how well the emotional body is balanced. If you are experiencing emotional stress, anger, depression or fear, even eating the best foods cannot prevent poisoning the body. These emotions can result in diarrhea, constipation, vomiting, indigestion and heartburn.

Regeneration must be accomplished at all levels of the Being, which includes the mind, body and soul.

The Healing removes the buildup of distorted energy patterns relating to thoughts, judgments, fears, etc. After the slate has been cleaned, two powerful tools to aid the regeneration and rejuvenation of the body are the *Harmonic Vibrational Essences* and *Soul Breathing* (both discussed later in this book).

I Choose to Be in a Safe Place at All Times

Understanding that you can now manifest your own reality through the desire of your thoughts, there are many interesting options that you may wish to consider.

Ann Marie and I "choose to be in a safe place at all times." For this to manifest into a reality, you must truly believe that what you have asked for, you have received. Your belief system becomes your reality. This has been demonstrated to us on many occasions. Allow me to share a few.

It was during the morning rush-hour traffic that I was driving with my mother toward San Francisco. As we approached the Golden Gate Bridge, there was a tunnel we had to pass through. Automobiles were bumper to bumper and traveling at high speeds. We were traveling in a fast lane with cars on both sides. Just before entering the tunnel, immediately ahead of us several cars began to spin out, crashing into each other and into the walls of the tunnel in one solid mass extending from one side of the tunnel to the other.

There was nowhere to go except into the wall of cars immediately ahead. Mother gasped as she tried to react, putting her hands onto the dashboard to brace herself. There was no time to apply the brakes, nor did it ever enter my thoughts. I only knew that I was safe and that no harm would befall us. In that instant, the cars directly ahead opened as if it were the parting of the waters of the Red Sea. Rather than hit the brakes, I pressed the accelerator to the floor and sped through the opening and beyond the reeling mass of automobiles in the tunnel. In the rear view mirror I saw the vehicles close immediately behind us, once again crashing into each other. Mother's hands had hardly touched the dashboard when she exclaimed, "What happened?" It had all happened so fast.

I smiled and replied, "It's okay, Mom, we're safe."

❖   ❖   ❖   ❖   ❖

While traveling to do our workshops in a motor home, Ann Marie and I parked the vehicle next to the home of an acquaintance, which was surrounded with mature pine trees. We pulled in just as a storm broke loose with 70-mile-per-hour winds and driving rain. There wasn't much for us to do except wait out the storm, and we were thankful that we were secure in the motor home.

Suddenly, we heard the loud and long sound of a tree breaking and falling. We held our breath, anticipating its fall. The tree hit the motor home with such an impact that the vehicle bounced completely off the ground, almost throwing us out of our seats. We sat there in the dark considering what to do next. Finally, after determining that there was no water leaking through the roof, I said, "I have no intention of going out in the storm. I will wait until morning to survey the damage."

After the storm had passed and the sun was shining, I cautiously opened the door to assess the damage. The fifty-foot tree had hit the ridge of the roof near the side door with such force the tree had broken into three separate parts. Two were lying on either side of the door, and had bounced in such a manner that neither had touched the motor home. I climbed the ladder to see what damage had been done to the antenna and other equipment mounted on top, and found to my surprise that the tree split upon impact and the top third of the tree had completely catapulted up and over the vehicle without touching its roof. The only damage was a three-inch crack in the paint on the surface where the tree had hit. Even then, it had not broken through the fiberglass.

❖   ❖   ❖   ❖   ❖

Ann Marie, riding with a friend, was attending a meeting for the day. That evening one of the participants left the meeting and noticed that the rear tire on Ann Marie's friend's car was flat, but being in a hurry, did not take the time to return and advise them.

Later they drove the thirty miles home unaware of the problem. The next morning, Ann Marie's friend received a phone call from the person who had noticed the flat tire, asking if they had arrived home safely, "considering the tire problem." Surprised, she responded, "What tire problem?" She rushed out to find that the tire was indeed flat, but no damage was apparent, nor did it appear to have been driven in that condition.

Angels

by ann marie

We may have to be brought to our knees before we will reach out for help; and that is exactly what happened to me. My experience with multiple sclerosis taught me about love. Sometimes the hardest lessons bring the greatest gifts.

I had separated from the love within. I had forgotten who I was. I was lost and lonely. Now as I reached out to God and asked for help, I began to feel the presence of the Angels. As they entered my life I felt a smile inside that I had not felt in a long time. I remembered playing with the Angels as a child; but the reality of the world around me took precedence over my invisible friends, and I was forced to "grow up." When I invited the Angels back into my life, I discovered they had never left my side. The Angels are to God like the elves are to Santa Claus — they are everywhere, and they love to be kept busy. They wanted to help me and were just waiting for me to listen.

There is nothing more pathetic than a bored Angel.

The Angels helped me to remember who I was and what I was capable of doing. They did all kinds of wonderful things for me. They would whisper in my ear and give me encouragement. Did you ever have a thought go through your mind that you *knew* didn't come from you? That's probably an Angel speaking to you, encouraging you, loving you, sharing new insights.

The Angels orchestrate situations and events —you know, those chance "coincidences." After awhile you begin to recognize that the coincidences become too coincidental not to be orchestrated by someone.

Imagine the fun the Angels must have making sure your car doesn't start so you are five minutes late to a meeting and you just happen to meet an old friend walking through the door. A friend you haven't seen in years. And now you discover that you never really knew the person, but she has dreams and visions just like yours. Or you are caught in a traffic jam and you hear that little voice inside say "turn right here" and you find yourself facing the most incredible double rainbow you have ever seen in your life reflected in a pond you had forgotten was there.

Moments that remind you of the magnificence of the Creator, moments that remind you of the vastness of the universe, moments that remind you that all things in creation are important.

Have you met the Angels around you? They are always there. The Angels are like the stars. Sometimes we don't see them because the clouds get in the way, but they are always there.

Angels come in all shapes and sizes. Close your eyes and visualize what the Angels around you might look like. Give yourself the freedom to accept whatever comes into your mind. Talk to them and let them assist you on your journey. The more you acknowledge their presence, the more you will see. They will begin to plan and scheme special events in your life, like having you drive thirty miles with a flat tire just to remind you that you are protected at all times.

You will be in a safe place at all times –

when you believe it.

Invisible Friends

Constant companions
embracing me in the wings of love
watching
never judging

Whispering sweetly in my ear
opening my eyes
to see the beauty of God's creation
and the perfection of my existence

Comforting me
with their sweet song of peace
reminding me of things forgotten
and my divinity

Waiting to be acknowledged
to have their deeds recognized and seen
to have their Love received in every way
to fulfill their destiny

A Visit from My Grandmother

Marie sat across the table sipping her tea. After a moment she said, "Rich, I can remember it as if happened yesterday. It was as real as you are. I stood barefooted, looking out of the kitchen window. I remember that I was wearing black shorts and a white blouse. It was a beautiful, warm summer day and my parents had gone shopping. It would be nice, I thought, to surprise them and make something for dinner. Spaghetti was one of my favorite dishes and I began to assemble the ingredients.

"Just then the doorbell rang. I was delighted to see that my grandmother had come to visit me. I had always been her favorite grandchild and we had always gotten along so well together. I gave her a big hug and a kiss. It had been so long since I had seen her and we had so much to talk about.

"She sat in Dad's chair at the kitchen table as I busied myself preparing the dinner. I recall that she was wearing a dark blue dress with a pretty white pattern running through it. There was a matching blue hat, and I loved her white gloves and the beautiful brooch she wore around her neck. I can still smell the fragrance of her perfume. It was as though she had just come from Easter services. I remember every detail.

"I was excited. I had turned sixteen and told Grandmother about all the things that had happened since we had last been together. I had passed the driving test and now had my drivers license, and there were many places that I could go and things that I could do.

"Twenty minutes had passed when Grandmother informed me that she had to leave. I said, 'Please stay. Mom and Dad will be home soon, and I know they would like to see you.'

"'Really, I must go,' she replied.

"I gave her another hug and a kiss and saw her to the door. 'I'll see you again soon,' she said as she turned and walked out the door.

"I returned to the stove and began stirring the spaghetti sauce when a thought occurred to me. I stood there stunned as I realized that Grandmother had died three years before. I ran to the door and into the driveway to see where she had gone, but there was no one there."

Marie sat looking into her teacup, then again at me. "Rich, I want to say that I had a vision, but to me it was as real as you and I are now. I could see the fly buzzing around the kitchen, the spaghetti sauce spattering as I worked with it. I could count every thread in Grandmother's dress and feel her warmth as I embraced her."

✧   ✧   ✧   ✧   ✧

Frequently during my workshops I will turn to my audience and ask, "Let me see a show of hands. How many of you have had an experience that we call psychic? It might be as subtle as knowing who is on the phone before you pick it up, or who is on the other side of the door before you open it. It may be a loved one who has crossed over and has returned to visit you, or an Angel that has appeared to bring you a message." Eighty to ninety percent raise their hands. Many have had such experiences, but most choose not to talk of them because others may not understand.

I do not believe that Marie's experience was a vision.

There are no unnatural or supernatural phenomena,

only very large gaps in our knowledge of what is natural.

We should strive to fill those gaps of ignorance.

—Edgar D. Mitchell, Apollo 14 astronaut

My Story

by ann marie

It was midafternoon when I awoke, the house was still and the only sound was the cold wind whistling through the pine trees outside my window. The chill that penetrated through me reminded me of the empty feeling in my heart.

It was a cold January day in the year 1982. For seven days I had been in bed, unable to do much of anything for myself. Engulfed in hopelessness, I searched for an answer by going back over the past.

For years I had been aware that something was wrong. I was tired all the time and pushed myself incessantly. There wasn't enough time to be tired or sick. The elusive symptoms were hard to identify: a little dizziness, fleeting numbness and constant fatigue were all symptoms the doctors couldn't explain. The reports were always the same: "You are in perfect health," they said. Rather than being labeled a hypochondriac, I stopped complaining and accepted this as part of life.

I was overwhelmed with the stress of the last few years: My father had cancer and died; my mother had conquered cancer; my son had undergone major surgery; my daughter had broken her arm and leg; and we had moved into a new home.

I remember the first major attack, which occurred on a hot summer day. Numbness crept down the left side of my body until my whole side was totally affected. There were several medical tests but no answers. The doctor said, "Go home and don't worry." Now I ask you, how does anyone in this situation go home and not worry? I knew something had to be wrong.

The numbness started to recede, then it came on the other side. There were more tests, and still no answers. A variety of symptoms came and went for several months. Then at the end of a four-day hospital stay, the doctor entered my room to announce that I had multiple sclerosis. I was so happy I could have hugged him. For the first time in years I had confirmation that I wasn't a hypochondriac! It wasn't all in my head! I really did have something organically wrong with me.

I sat there with this big smile on my face, and with the innocence of a child said, "Okay, now that we know what this is, what do we do to get rid of it?" I'll never forget the look in his eyes. He didn't know how to tell me there was nothing he could do. Naturally, I didn't believe that, so I went looking for answers. After seeing several doctors, I finally understood their prognosis: that there is no known cause, no cure and no *hope* for multiple sclerosis. The only advice I was given was to "go home, keep doing what you are doing, live the best life you can, and call me so I can help you with the different symptoms as they come along."

As I lay listening to the wind, I realized that I had family and friends who loved me, but I felt alone and defeated. The enemy, multiple sclerosis, appeared to be winning the war. My body was continuously degenerating. My right leg was totally dead to feeling and was atrophying, the calf half the size of my left leg. My left leg was going numb. It was becoming increasingly difficult to walk and almost impossible to climb steps. My balance had been off from the beginning, and I had forgotten what stability was like. The right side of my head was numb and it was creeping down into my face, at times affecting my tongue, and speech became difficult and slurred. The coordination of my hands and arms would come and go. There were bad days and better days, but I no longer had what I would call good days.

It was a personal battle between myself and "it," and there seemed to be no one who could truly help me fight this enemy. I called out to God: "Is there no one out there who can help me? Must I stand alone, defenseless against this enemy? Are there no weapons for me to use? Is there no path of retreat? Dear God, I can't go on like this. This is no longer living, but merely existing. Please, Lord, I know that you know how to heal my body. Show me the way and I'll share it with the world. I place my life in your hands, for I can no longer go on without hope." And in that moment of despair, I planned my suicide.

Message of Hope

I awoke the next morning to the ringing of the phone. Someone I had met a few weeks ago was calling to tell me she had been praying and received a message from the Lord to call and tell me that multiple sclerosis could be conquered. She didn't know how, she didn't have any specific answers, just that it was possible.

My heart soared as I placed the phone back on its cradle. I would have danced if I could. I had just received the greatest gift of all — *hope*. I knew God would show me the way to restore my body by providing the tools to use in my war. I knew there could be many hard battles, but I would win the war.

The cold wind blew through the pines outside my window as I snuggled in my warm bed. The despair in my heart melted in the warmth of God's love as it flooded through my Being. I was no longer alone in my struggle against this formidable enemy. Somehow God would guide me, and I would follow as best I could.

In the beginning there was very little information to go on, only hope and faith. I began reading the one book I had on health: the Bible. I knew that if God said multiple sclerosis could be conquered, there must be something about health in the scriptures. I picked up the Bible and allowed it to fall open by itself. Wherever my eyes fell, there was a passage on health and healing.

After awhile I realized that a blue sparkle would twinkle on the page beside a line of particular importance. I was amazed at the amount of information and beautiful guidance I was receiving. At the same time, I began to receive information from a variety of sources. It was as though the dam had opened and I was standing in the flood. People sent me articles of people known to have conquered multiple sclerosis. As I read about their success, I knew I too had a chance. For if just one person had conquered multiple sclerosis, so could another.

My Quest for Health

Within a short period of time I realized that life as I had known it would be changed. With hope in my heart, I began looking at myself, my life and all things around me from a new perspective. It was a new beginning. Each day was the "first day of the rest of my life." Each day I was laying the groundwork for my future. I wanted to create balance and harmony in all parts of my life – physical, emotional and spiritual. With faith that God would guide me to the information and the people who could help me, I began my quest.

My thirst for knowledge could not be quenched. Each answer would lead to more questions. The more I discovered, the more I realized how much more I wanted to know. My search led me through medical journals and research from all over the world, books about multiple sclerosis, health, natural food, exercise and stress reduction.

I had been told that the body replaces itself every seven years, except for the nerve cells. I set my goals for a seven-year plan. (New research now shows that the body replaces itself every eleven months.) I believed that if I raised my total level of health, the disease within my body would not progress. I would have been satisfied if I could just halt the progression of the disease, because then I would know that I was in control, rather than the problem being in control of me.

To my delight, as my health improved the process of degeneration stopped and the symptoms began to disappear. In the beginning there were many ups and downs. But I did not lose heart, for somewhere deep down inside of me, I knew it would be okay if I lost a few battles. I was in this for the long haul, and I planned to win the war. Each time I struggled in a battle, I would survey where I was, make necessary revisions in my battle plan and launch the best offensive that I knew at the time. As time went on, I became wiser and more aware of what I needed to do to stay in balance and harmony. My battles became easier and I became more victorious. Yes, I have discovered that the body truly is capable of totally healing itself.

So here is my message to you: There is HOPE. Hope for a better way of life. I share with you my story and the knowledge of what has worked for myself and others. You and you alone are responsible for your health and the course of your life. Every day you make decisions that affect every aspect of your life. If it is your desire to increase your health, happiness and longevity, I offer you this information to help you conquer your challenges, stop the progression of degeneration and change your life.

The Body Is Capable of Healing Itself

My body has been symptom-free for several years. It is my belief that God created us in such a magnificent way that if we provide a positive internal and external environment, our body is capable of healing itself. A marvelous blueprint of perfection lies within our cells. We constantly see proof of this. For example, if you cut your finger and you wash it, put antiseptic on it and apply a band-aid, in a few days it will be healed. However, if you keep getting it dirty and cracking it open, it could take weeks to heal. The only difference in the ability to heal is the environment provided.

It is my belief that God created us in such a magnificent way

that if we provide a positive internal and external environment,

our body is capable of healing itself.

The human body is constantly changing. It is composed of 100 trillion cells, of which approximately one billion replace themselves each hour. As long as we remain in harmony and balance physically, emotionally, mentally and spiritually, we provide a regenerative environment.

Imagine, if every person on the Earth were in a place of peace, harmony, love and joy within themselves and with others, what kind of a world would we have? If every cell in your body were in peace, harmony, love and joy within itself and with every other cell, what kind of a body would you have?

When we were created, we were given one law: the Law of Free-Will Choice. We make choices every minute of every day. As situations arise, we choose to do something or we choose to do nothing. Either way, we make a choice. In every situation there are usually three choices. Are the aspects of your life bringing you happiness and joy? As you make choices in joy, new directions and pathways become visible that you never saw before.

Imagine that you just received your drivers license and you have been offered a brand new automobile that you can drive anywhere you choose. There is only one stipulation: This will be the only automobile that you will ever be able to own. How would you choose to care for this vehicle? Would you give it tender, loving care? Or would you run it until it started to give you problems and *then* begin to think about its care and maintenance? Would you follow your inner guidance, or would you be swayed by what your family, neighbors or society directed you to do? Would you aspire to maintain high-quality service indefinitely, or would you just sit back and let whatever happens, happen?

You are living in a vehicle known as your body. If you are tired of the condition of your vehicle or the road you are on, you can choose to change. Remember, the choice is always yours.

If every person on the Earth were in a place of peace, harmony,

love and joy within themselves and with others,

_what kind of a world would we have?

If every cell in your body were in peace, harmony,

love and joy within themselves and with every other cell,

what kind of a body would you have?

My Search Continues

It has been a beautiful experience to watch my body's transformation. For years I studied health from many perspectives. I returned to college and received a Master of Science degree in Nutrition, then furthered my education by gathering additional training and knowledge in biochemistry, vibratory essences, homeopathy, herbology, color therapy, Reiki, craniosacral therapy, polarity therapy, orthobionomy, kinesiology and other studies on healing.

After years of searching I was still looking for the elusive answers to the simplicity of healing. I was able to stabilize my health, with only a few minor symptoms remaining, by staying on a strict program I had developed that consisted of a whole, natural diet and hundreds of dollars worth of food supplements and herbs each month.

The success of my wellness program was obvious, and many came to ask what I had done. Looking for a simple answer or a magic pill, one person wanted me to give her the name of my doctor so that she could go to him and get the same help I had gotten. She had a difficult time accepting where my help had come from. Most wanted someone to take responsibility for their health and remove the burden from them. They were not aware that they had created their disease and only they could remove it.

Each day I meditate and I follow my inner guidance. As my body was healing, I continued to look for more answers. I believed that a person should be able to maintain and build their health in an atmosphere of joy and without jeopardizing the health of their pocketbook.

I had a vision of being with someone during a therapy session, when Jesus walked into the room, placed his hands on mine and said, "Remember, only Love heals." Later he stood beside me, placed his hands next to mine, and said, "It is this simple." My friend felt his hands upon her and received a Healing. During my meditations he said, "Remember, all knowledge, through all time, exists within the soul. You must go within and remember."

I was determined to know the simple answers of healing with love, to continue to enhance my health and to assist others.

My Philosophy of Wellness

by ann marie

After weeks of meditation, with the intent of bringing forth the simplicity of Healing, the following philosophy of wellness emerged.

- ♥ There is one disease: *low-level wellness.*

- ♥ Everyone is on a continuum of wellness.

- ♥ At the midpoint is the absence of symptoms.

- ♥ As you move up the continuum, you raise your level of wellness.

- ♥ As you move down the continuum, you lower your level of wellness.

- ♥ As you lower your level of wellness, symptoms occur that relate to the toxic emotions, toxic chemicals and genetic weaknesses within your systems.

- ♥ What determines where you are on this continuum is the *flow and amplitude of your life-force energy.*

- ♥ As you raise your level of wellness by increasing the flow and amplitude of your life-force energy, you awaken the body's ability to heal itself.

The Key to Healing

is in Receiving and Retaining the Vibrations of Love.

Each individual cell in your body has a consciousness, and it is time to begin raising that consciousness. You alone are responsible for this task.

Think of the Earth as a Being with trillions of human cells upon it. They have been separated from the Love of the Creator through judgment and fear passed on through generation after generation, and now it is time for each soul to return to its connection to the Creator. The same is true for each one of the cells in your body.

As you open the mind, the memory within each cell opens to the concept that it too is part of the Creator. It automatically begins to fill itself with love.

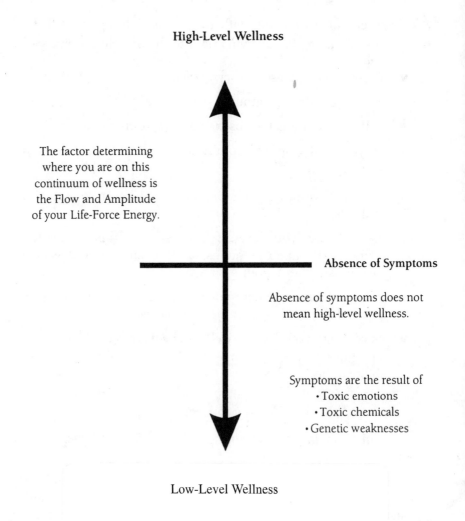

High-Level Wellness

The factor determining where you are on this continuum of wellness is the Flow and Amplitude of your Life-Force Energy.

Absence of Symptoms

Absence of symptoms does not mean high-level wellness.

Symptoms are the result of
• Toxic emotions
• Toxic chemicals
• Genetic weaknesses

Low-Level Wellness

There is only one disease - Low-Level Wellness

The simplicity of Healing

is that you can awaken the cells of your body

to receive and retain the Vibrations of Love.

The body's ability to heal itself is directly proportionate to the amount of love each cell is able to receive and retain.

Life Potential

♥ The cells and systems of the body begin to degenerate as the distorted vibrations of fear begin to accumulate throughout the being.

♥ To protect themselves from distorted energies, the cells create walls, which restrict the flow of life-force energy.

♥ As the life-force energy decreases, the cells begin to degenerate.

♥ If the life-force energy is completely depleted, the cells die.

♥ When love comes their way, they are not open to receive. They have blocked the very love that can save their life.

♥ As the creator and overseer of your body, it is up to you to clear out the blockages of energy and to reawaken the consciousness of the cells to accept the pure vibrations of love that come their way.

♥ As life-force energy increases, the cells are able to regenerate and rejuvenate themselves.

♥ By raising the resonance of love within our Being high enough, the body can restore itself to its fullest potential and literally reverse the aging process.

The Key to Healing is

in Receiving and Retaining the Vibrations of Love.

Negotiating Peace

Everything in your world is a mirror for you. All you have to do is look around and you will see exactly what is happening inside the world of your body. Turn on the television and see what happens to a country that is at war. Most of us have been living in a body that has been at war since conception. We have been inundated with emotions and thought patterns handed down through the generations, then we enter a world filled with fear, judgment and conditional love. Is it little wonder that our bodies degenerate and age?

If you were the head of a nation at war, would you first choose to negotiate peace, or try to rebuild the country? I have watched many people struggling for years to rebuild their country without first negotiating peace.

Through the Healing you have negotiated peace in your country and now you are faced with the task of rebuilding.

If you were the head of a nation at war,

which would you choose to do first?

Negotiate peace –

or try to rebuild the country?

A key to raising your level of wellness is to

♥ Eliminate or decrease those frequencies that deplete your life-force energy.

♥ Increase those frequencies that enhance your life-force energy.

All things contain either the pure frequencies of Love or the distorted frequencies of fear.

After starting on my natural health program, I developed an inner awareness of what, when, and how much food to put into my body. I knew instinctively what to avoid and what things my body wanted. I have discovered that you too can access this inner knowing. There are many techniques that you may use. We have already discussed kinesiology; a second method is penduling (dowsing).

Penduling

Everything is energy and all energy resonates at a frequency. The brain processes everything as a frequency and then categorizes, files and compares it so that we may have knowledge of the world we live in. The life-force energy system within each person has an individual frequency which all other frequencies can affect in one of three ways:

- ♥ They can enhance your energy,
- ♥ They can deplete your energy
- ♥ They are compatible (will neither benefit nor deplete your energies).

As you increase those frequencies that will enhance you and eliminate those that deplete you, you will raise your level of wellness and your symptoms will begin to disappear.

Penduling, dowsing with a pendulum, is using the "life-magnet" that is present throughout the body to determine how specific frequencies affect you. A pendulum works with the body's polarity system, creating either a resistance or an attraction, similar to demonstrations with magnets. When two like poles are brought together, they repel; opposite poles attract and are drawn together.

A pendulum can be anything that hangs and swings freely, such as a chain or string with a weight on the end. Using the life-force energy that goes up the left arm, across the shoulders and down the right arm, your brain will send out different energy patterns. These patterns can be used to indicate the enhancement or incompatibility of any substance. This provides a valuable tool to access your inner knowing and assist you in creating a positive internal and external environment for your Healing. It is like receiving a computer printout from your brain.

With wrist bent, hold string or chain between thumb, index finger and middle finger.

Left hand = Negative (-) South pole _____
Right hand = Positive (+) North pole _____
Middle finger (North pole)   = Positive (+) Pattern: _____
Pointer finger (South pole)   = Negative (-) Pattern: _____
Thumb =   Neutral Pattern: _____

Become aware of the life-force energy in your arm circuit. Start by holding your hands (palms facing each other) about four inches apart, then swiftly but gently move them in and out in a bouncing motion, as though you intend to clap your hands, but do not allow your hands to touch each other. Do this until you feel the energy building between them. This energy may feel like a tingling, a soft breeze, a warmth between your hands. Different people perceive it differently. This energy is sufficient to create the movement of your pendulum.

Now hold the chain or string of your pendulum between the positive, negative and neutral poles of your dominant hand (if you are right-handed, use your right hand). Raise your elbow comfortably away from your body; your hand should drop down so that your three fingers holding the indicator will point straight down.

Hold the indicator above your POSITIVE (+) middle finger of the opposite hand (it has a positive magnetic charge) and say, "This is my positive pattern." Your focus should be on your finger, not on the indicator. You may want to write down exactly which direction the indicator is swinging for each of the patterns.

Next, hold the indicator over your NEGATIVE (-) index finger and say, "This is my negative pattern."

Repeat this procedure with the NEUTRAL thumb.

Once you have (consistently) recognized what your personal patterns are, you are ready to determine if the frequencies of different substances are compatible with, or will enhance, your body's biomagnetic frequency.

To check an item (if you hold the pendulum in your right hand), hold the object in your left hand (or hold your left hand over the object) and state, "This is compatible with my body." If you receive a negative pattern (showing you that it is incompatible), you may wish to avoid this substance. If the pattern is positive, it is compatible. Now check to see if it will enhance your energy by stating, "This enhances my body." If you receive a positive pattern, you may wish to utilize this substance to enhance your life-force energy. When you check foods or supplements and receive a positive response, you may wish to check for the quantity that will enhance you the most.

Example: You have just found that cranberry juice will enhance your body. Now ask, "How many glasses would enhance me in one day?" The indicator should start moving in your positive pattern as you slowly count: "one, two, three" etc. As soon as the pattern changes, repeat the last number you said. You should get a negative response, so the amount would be the number prior to that. (If you received a negative to the number three, drinking two glasses would enhance you.) You may choose to state the question differently to be sure, such as "Two glasses of cranberry juice a day will enhance me." *Also* ask if it is better to drink the juice at a specific time of day and with or between meals.

Note: This tool may be used effectively for the purpose for which it is taught. It may take time before your indicator begins to move. Relax. Check where your elbow is. Refocus and try it again. Do not focus so hard that you hold your breath. This will stop the movement of the pendulum. Breathe. Some people believe that I am making the pendulum move because my hand moves. Remember, the energy pattern is coming down your arm from your brain, so if you relax your hand enough you will be able to feel the energy actually move your hand. Forcing your hand to stay still will stop the energy flow, stopping the pendulum. Relax.

The frequencies that affect you come from everything in your world: the food you eat, the water you drink, the thoughts you think, etc. A negative frequency can affect you if it is stronger than the amplitude of your life-force energy. As you raise your level of wellness, those things that you could not tolerate before may again be acceptable.

As you begin to distinguish how different energies affect you, you may receive what appear to be conflicting data. For example, a portion of meat may enhance you at noon but deplete your energies in the evening. A slice of bread may enhance you on one day but deplete you the rest of the week. Keeping a journal for several weeks will help you recognize your patterns.

There is one substance that affects your health more than any other. You wear it from head to toe twenty-four hours a day. If it is depleting to your life-force energy, it gradually lowers your level of wellness little by little throughout your lifetime. If you already have a low level of wellness, it will sabotage your ability to regenerate your body. This substance is your *laundry detergent*. Therefore, this is one of the first things you want to check. You will want to check all substances that you put in or on your body. Here is a suggested list:

- ♥ Laundry detergent
- ♥ Water and beverages
- ♥ All food throughout the day
- ♥ Food supplements
- ♥ Toiletries and makeup
- ♥ Your clothing
- ♥ Sheets and blankets
- ♥ Colors

Color has a powerful effect on you. The color that you wear closest to your hypothalamus (a gland located in your head) has the greatest influence. A wonderful, inexpensive form of color therapy is to have several different-colored pillowcases from which to choose so that each night you can find the one that most enhances you.

The Source of All Knowledge

There is no new knowledge or old knowledge. All knowledge already exists.

Let us say that I take a picture frame, and inside this frame I find the sum total of the Creator (or God as we refer to God, the Source, the Creator of all things). Is not God "all Love"? Is not God "all knowledge"? Then all knowledge already exists. Our ability to access it depends on how fully conscious we are.

A hundred years ago our experts said it was impossible to build an atom bomb or create a glass tube that would transmit a picture around the world. It was impossible. It couldn't be done. Today if you were to ask you would be told that half the kids in the neighborhood can make an A-bomb in their basement. Now it is considered old knowledge.

Our awareness keeps shifting. When you work with your intuitive self or a pendulum, understand that *all knowledge already exists.* You are tapping into universal knowledge. What you must determine is, Where is this information coming from? Integrity is essential. I suggest that you first repeat the following affirmation.

I will accept only that Knowledge which comes in Light and Love
and from my Highest Source.

Harmonic Vibrational Essences

The universal language of love is expressed in the harmonic vibrations of light, sound and color. We experience the vibrations of Universal Love whenever we step into a beautiful cathedral, temple or chapel, watch a beautiful sunset, or feel our heart being touched by love. Using a specially selected method of energy transfer, these pure frequencies of love are transferred into liquid, producing the Harmonic Vibrational Essences.

The concept of energy transfer is all around us. Did you ever wonder how sound reaches your brain and has a meaning; how emotion produces a physiological effect on the body; how the picture gets onto the film in your camera; or how light can be turned into a laser? Energy is in constant motion and can be perceived and utilized in many ways. Imagine a beam of red laser light being projected across the darkened skies. We can all see it, and it can be controlled in certain ways to cut through a piece of steel or operate on the human eye. Where did this energy come from? How did they put it into a workable form? If you took it into a laboratory, you would find it has no chemical composition. It is just energy.

Universal Love: The most powerful energy in the universe. When we speak of the vibrations of love, we are speaking of powerful positive energies that are capable of transmuting distorted energies and bringing them back into harmonious balance. The vibrations of Universal Love are expressed as the full spectrum of light, sound and color.

The Harmonic Vibrational Essences enhance your Being with the resonance of the universal language of love. They are preserved in a base of pure oxygenated crystalline water and come in one-ounce bottles. These essences can

♥ build and nourish life-force energy systems;

♥ rejuvenate and regenerate physical cells and systems;

♥ renew the resonance of love at the cellular level;

♥ transmute the distorted frequencies in your life-force energy system back to the pure frequencies of love;

♥ restore disharmonic patterns back to harmony;

♥ clear and release blockages in energy flow;

♥ strengthen the positive attributes on all levels of the subtle and physical bodies; and

♥ assist the body's resonance to return to its most perfected state.

Let me introduce you to the Harmonic Vibrational Essences.

Rainbow Essence

A Spark of Life

restores the water of the Earth with the resonance of Love

rejuvenating and regenerating my cells and systems

There is Peace and Harmony

as Rainbow Light twinkles in the heart of my Being

The Rainbow Essence of Universal Love restores the spark of life to water. By transforming the fluids of the body, it caresses the cells with love, transmutes toxins, restores systems, rejuvenates and rehydrates the skin, and accelerates nutritional absorption into the cells, thus enhancing total health and well-being.

Note: A major concern of the 1994 International Dowsers Convention in England was that they could find no "living" water left on the surface of the Earth.

To renew the Spark of Life in water, add to your container of water the following amounts of the essence to make Rainbow Water for internal and external use:

♥ Drinking and cooking: Add 2 drops to 1 gallon.

♥ Bath or hot tub: Add 2 or 3 drops.

♥ Laundry: Add 2 drops per washload (Note: By adding Rainbow Essence to your tub of water, your laundry will be energized, thus protecting you from electromagnetic rays in the atmosphere).

♥ Watering and misting plants: 2 drops per gallon of water.

♥ When feeling sluggish, put 1 or 2 drops under tongue.

♥ Body Mist: Add 2 or 3 drops per 2 oz. Rainbow Water in an atomizer.

♥ Fruits and vegetables: Add 2 drops to a sink of water and soak for 5 minutes.

♥ Food supplements: Add 2 drops per glass of water.

Angelic Essence

As the song of the Angels
fills my heart with Joy
Love emanates through my Being
Awakening the Healer Within

An Angelic Essence of Universal Love enhances the flow and amplitude of life-force energy, thus raising the resonance of love, releasing distorted energy patterns, restoring the immune system and increasing life potential.

♥ To renew the full spectrum of life to your Being, add 2 drops of Angelic Essence to water and drink 3 times a day.

♥ To renew the full spectrum of life to your foods and beverages, place 2 or 3 drops of Angelic Essence directly on your plate at mealtime or in each dish being served, as well as your beverage. (Optional: May be added to Rainbow Water or on foods rinsed in Rainbow Water.)

♥ To renew the full spectrum of life to a physical distress, apply topically.

♥ To renew the full spectrum of life to your subtle-energy body, add 5 drops to 2 ounces of water (preferably Rainbow Water) in an atomizer bottle and spritz your hands, feet, and aura as often as desired. Especially refreshing at bedtime for a good night's sleep. Also spritz directly onto areas of physical distress.

♥ Add 2 to 4 drops of Angelic Essence to everything that goes onto or into the body — shampoo, body lotion, face cream, hair spray, etc.

Goddess Essence

Inner strength awakens the power within

bringing forth the Desires of my Heart

in Divine Love

The Goddess Essence of Universal Love emanates through the being, renewing the resonance of love, removing boundaries and limitations, reestablishing inner strength, balancing masculine and feminine energies and restoring peace and harmony.

- ♥ To restore harmony and inner strength, place 2 to 5 drops under the tongue as often as desired (especially before meditating and at bedtime).

- ♥ To reduce cravings, place 2 or 3 drops under the tongue as often as desired (especially with caffeinated drinks or chocolate).

Ascension Essence

Ascend from fear and judgment

into Unconditional Love

The Ascension Essence of Universal Love is the essence of transition and change that empowers the movement of the old into the new; transmutes negative energies; allows your creativity to burst fort; opens the door to greater understanding and a new sense of freedom; and brings forth the essence of your inner being into the reality of your world.

♥ Wear an Essendulum* filled with Ascension Essence to surround yourself with love.

♥ Place 2 to 5 drops under tongue or in water daily.

Essendulum: A beautiful pendant containing a glass vial enclosed in wood carved out of scraps from the rainforest. (Proceeds from the Essendulum have preserved over 14,000 acres of rainforest.) Wearing an Essendulum containing Ascension Essence shields and stabilizes your energy field against environmental frequencies and expands the flow and amplitude of your life-force energy. This protection dramatically decreases the physical, emotional and mental stress in your life.

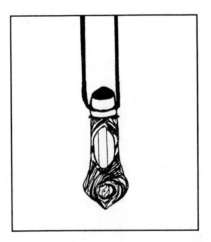

The Essendulum

Experience the Essences

To experience the effect the essences have on your life-force energy system and the life-force energy of other substances, make the following tests.

♥ Rainbow Essence

Place 2 drops of Rainbow Essence in a gallon of water. Taste the water before and after you add it. Take a piece of fruit (apple slice, grape, etc.), *cut* it in half and soak one half in Rainbow Water for 5 minutes. Ttaste the difference.

♥ Angelic Essence

Feeling the energy between your hands, pay special attention to the changes in volume and strength as you mist your aura with an atomizer containing 5 drops of Angelic Essence for every 2 ounces of Rainbow Water.

Try the following taste tests:

1. Take a sip from a full glass of water, paying attention to the taste. Add 2 drops of Angelic Essence, wait 15 seconds, and notice the change in taste. (It is especially noticeable in municipal water.)

2. Repeat the above test using a can of your favorite carbonated beverage, coffee or wine.

3. Repeat the above taste test with a dish of food. (Just add 2 drops to the dish; the resonance will permeate through all of the food.) Pay special attention to the taste before and after, how it feels in your mouth, and how afterwards a small amount of food will satisfy your appetite.

♥ Goddess Essence

Place 2 or 3 drops of Goddess Essence under your tongue, then notice the smile of radiance expanding through your Being and your renewed sense of peace and inner harmony.

♥ Pyramid

Position the four Harmonic Pyramid bottles within a room. Be aware of the change in the air and note any other changes. After awhile, pick up and remove one of the four bottles. The instant that you move it, the etheric pyramid will collapse. Notice the shift in the energy. (Description follows)

Harmonic Pyramid Energy

A "transactive" pyramid

allows for transition through action

allowing Free-Will Choice

to assist you in your transition

and achieve balance in the equilibrium of Love

within your Being.

By placing the four Harmonic Pyramid bottles in a square or rectangular pattern, an etheric pyramid is formed. The essence of life is enhanced in everything inside the pyramid: Air appears fresher, water becomes alive and plants "breathe." The etheric Harmonic Pyramid stabilizes energies, thus raising the vibrations of love within your Being; creating joy, peace and harmony; removing judgments and fears; and guiding you to an ever higher vibration of Unconditional Love. It allows transition to take place, guided by your inner Being. Each person will have individual experiences.

The Harmonic Pyramid Essence comes as a matched set of four bottles coded with a serial number and cannot be interchanged with any other set.

♥ House: Place one bottle at each of the four inside corners of your house/apartment or the four corners of your property; keep to a square or rectangular pattern.

♥ Portable Pyramid: You may carry an extra Harmonic Pyramid for your office, your automobile, etc.

♥ Office: Use the Pyramid for your own personal use only. Do not invade the privacy of others. If you own your business, you may place it on the four corners of your property or building. If you work in an office, place it in the four corners of your workspace.

♥ Automobile: Place it inside the four corners of your automobile. If there is a possibility of freezing, remove it.

♥ Therapy: Place around your work area or in the corners of your office.

♥ Meditation: Place the Pyramid around you while you meditate.

♥ Multiple Pyramids: Placing one Pyramid within another is an incredible experience. It multiples the energy. Place a Pyramid at the four corners of your property, home or room, then place a personal Pyramid around your workplace in your home, meditation or therapy space or around a loved one who may be ill. (Be sure you get their permission. You do not need permission from your children.)

**The Harmonic Pyramid Essences
are not for internal or external use on the body.
Use only as directed.**

Supporting the Immune System

The condition of the immune system is a major concern in our society today. Hospitals and doctors' offices are full of patients. The bottom line to health is the immune system. Almost everything affects it — your emotions, your diet, your environment. The Harmonic Essences have been a major part of my wellness program to support my immune system and raise my total level of wellness. I [ann marie] choose to use the following program.

Ascension Essence: To assist in the transition to high-level wellness,

- ♥ put 2 to 5 drops under the tongue or in drinking water daily;
- ♥ wear an Essendulum, which is filled with this Essence.

Angelic Essence: To restore the full spectrum of life,

- ♥ put 2 drops in water or beverages 3 times daily;
- ♥ put 2 drops on a plate or dish of food at mealtime;
- ♥ apply topically as desired.

Rainbow Essence: To renew the spark of life to the element of water,

- ♥ add 2 drops to 1 gallon of water for drinking and cooking;
- ♥ add 2 or 3 drops to a bath or hot tub;
- ♥ add 2 drops per washload of laundry (to add a strong positive energy force to clothes, bedding, etc);
- ♥ add 3 drops to a gallon of water for plants;
- ♥ add 2 drops to a sink of water to soak your fruits and vegetables;
- ♥ put 2 drops in the water you use to swallow your food supplements.

Goddess Essence: To balance the masculine/feminine energies,

- ♥ hold the bottle in your left hand while meditating;
- ♥ put 5 drops under your tongue before meditation and at bedtime.

Atomizer: To renew the full spectrum of life to the subtle energy body,

♥ add 5 drops Angelic Essence to 2 ounces of Rainbow Water in an atomizer bottle and spritz hands, feet and aura as often as desired (especially at bedtime for an excellent night's sleep). Also spritz directly onto areas of physical distress.

Harmonic Pyramid Essence: See earlier description.

Harmonic Notes

Pets (animals love these Essences, too):

♥ Rainbow Water soothes them in love, bringing about a re-newed peace and harmony. Use 2 drops per 1 gallon of water.

♥ Angelic Essence renews the full spectrum of life to their food. Add 1 drop for a cat or small dog, 2 for a large dog, 3 or 4 for a horse.

♥ To renew the full spectrum of life to their subtle energy body, use an atomizer. (Add 5 drops of Angelic Essence to 2 drops of Rainbow Water.)

✧ ✧ ✧ ✧ ✧

Environmental chemicals left me with severe chemical poison-ing. I was paralyzed and unable to walk, and I had severe reactions to prescription drugs. I began a program of Harmonic Essences. I improved rapidly and now work two full-time jobs (80 hours a week). — P.C.

✧ ✧ ✧ ✧ ✧

My friend has coped with drug and alcohol addictions plus mental illness for over thirteen years. Following a series of destruc-tive events, all drug-induced, he chose to withdraw from his addic-tions. Soon the withdrawal became more than he could bear. He called to say, "Either I come to your house or I go to the bar." I invited him over and placed 30 drops of Harmonic Essences in a cup of water. He drank it down and within a few minutes he became calm and rational. He also agreed to place some Essences on his infected tattoo, as he could barely lift his arm. He said it felt cooling, and he was able to lift his arm freely in fifteen minutes. I have used the Harmonic Essences many times in similar situations. The results are incredible. — S.Z., volunteer advocate for the mentally ill

✧   ✧   ✧   ✧   ✧

I use herbal products and am in good health. The Harmonic Essences take me over the peak. They bring a synthesis to whatever else I do. I add the Essences to my moisturizing lotion, and my face has a special glow. I ran out of them a month ago and I noticed that I no longer had that special glow. There is a subtle something that is missing when I don't use Harmonic Essences. It makes all the difference between just feeling okay, and feeling great, on top of the world. Harmonic Essences raise my level of joy, the inner feeling as well as the outer expression. I find that the Harmonic Essences fill in the gaps. — M.P.

✧   ✧   ✧   ✧   ✧

I am a massage therapist. An accident with a glue gun left a large amount of hot glue over my finger. The pain was excruciating. I grabbed my Harmonic Essences and poured it over my finger. Shortly after, the pain stopped, and the next day, with only a band-aid to cover the open flesh, I completed four massages with no pain. It healed rapidly. — C.Z.

✧   ✧   ✧   ✧   ✧

My sister, who has MS, was scheduled for her seventh intravenous ATCH intravenous treatment. She really dislikes them because they cause her to have many seizures and make her sick afterwards. I gave her some Harmonic Essences to take along with the treatment. She was elated because the treatment went so well. This time she experienced only a couple of mild seizures and felt quite good the entire time. — S.H.

Note: The following are animal testimonials. Animals, unlike humans, have no ego nor do they experience the placebo effect that can influence testimonies. What you see is what you get. Many feel animal testimonials are more valid than human ones.

I have a Belgian horse that had developed a large knot on his left front leg just above the hoof. He was irritable and difficult to approach. The veterinarian diagnosed it as "ringbone," with pinnacles that went down into the hoof. He said it was incurable and suggested that we take him to the "dog food factory." We began using a large dose of Harmonic Essences (after all, this was a 2000-pound horse), and soon he was no longer irritable and was easy to approach. In a month the big knot started to recede. In the following weeks there was a major change, and soon he was no longer limping. He now pulls the wagon in the parade. — L.S.

✧   ✧   ✧   ✧   ✧

We have about sixty horses in our stable, and use the Harmonics as well as supplements along with them. I am a firm believer in the Harmonic program, and I readily see the results not only in the healings, but in the animals' vitality, stamina and eagerness to work on the trail. It is an exciting product. — L.S.

✧   ✧   ✧   ✧   ✧

My dog (a Doberman) had been limping, holding his hind leg up for several weeks. I rubbed Harmonics freely on his rear quarter several times that evening. The next morning I was excited to see that my dog was running and bearing the full weight on his hind leg. — L.S.

Awakening to Your *

Whe are experiencing a journey on Earth in a vehicle known as a body. Through time, we have put up walls around our soul in such a way that our mental and physical bodies are now running our lives. The soul waits to be acknowledged and given permission to take charge. When the soul is ignored, we feel the pain of separation. Joy can exist only when the soul is allowed to express itself. Healing occurs when the soul is acknowledged.

The key to health is not found in some vitamin or herb, nor is it found in some outside source. It is found within every one of your 100 trillion cells. As you awaken the soul within each cell, it returns to its perfected state of being, allowing the radiance of love to ignite the eternal flame of life.

Perfection

Before we explore the concept of awakening the soul in each cell, we need to look at the concept of perfection. Perfection is not creating a perfect image for someone else. Perfection is expressing yourself in joy and in the perfection of your *Being*, not your image. You are perfect, you always have been and you always will be.

There is a basic need to be loved and accepted by others. We just want to be loved for who we are, for what we are. We want to be recognized as someone who is lovable, who is acceptable, who is good enough. We desire to be perfect, but are so busy judging ourselves that we create an image of what we believe society, our mate, our parents or our children expect us to be.

There was a time in my life when I was more carefree; then I became "responsible," and bought into the fears and judgments of others. Most of my choices were based on fear—fear of eating certain foods because they might make me ill, fearing that someone might not approve of what I was doing. I was even afraid of making

sion, fearing it might be the "wrong" choice.

At first we feel safe behind our cardboard image, protected by the walls and boundaries we have set; but soon we become prisoners within these walls, trapped by the image we have created and too afraid of the opinions and judgments of others to show our true self to the world. The walls become barriers to the very love we crave. These etheric walls begin to manifest into reality as the distorted frequencies of fear and judgment permeate into the physical body, setting up barriers of resistance in the life-force energy field.

As we understand that we are spiritual beings expressing ourselves in human form, we can put away our struggles and begin to play.

I see a world full of people sending love to others. But sending love to someone is seeing that person as less than perfect, in a state of need. If they would stop sending love and *start seeing the perfection in all things*, the world would heal itself.

When we see the perfection in another, we recognize the love that exists within them. We acknowledge that they have everything they need. This creates a shift in energy and allows the Universal Laws of Creative Manifestation to bring forth the desires of their heart.

"I see you (him / her) in perfection"

Mirrors

The picturesque view stirs my heart
feelings of another world
another place not quite remembered
wanting to remain in this state of Being
no turmoil
Not even wanting to breathe for fear of losing this essence
then taking a deep breath
allowing the feeling to penetrate deep within my Being
like merging into a beautiful painting
wondering why it isn't always like this
why we must go somewhere to get this feeling
why isn't it always with us

I know now what it is
it feels satisfied, full, not empty
this is the feeling of completeness, perfection
the beauty of nature is a mirror of our own perfection
and we remember who we are
we become one with the perfection of the Universe
so we feel complete, whole
how could there be more
there is no judgment here

As we turn and face the world we see another mirror
we perceive imperfection and we judge
since everything is reflected inward
we begin to feel incomplete
we struggle with our perceived imperfections
and the inner turmoil begins again

Thank God for reminders of our perfection
for moments like this
that some day will last forever
when we face the world and see only perfection
in all things
especially in ourselves

Receiving Love

Call forth a partner to stand before you. Now see yourself reaching out to hug that person, who has put up walls of protection, and "send" her love. The love cannot penetrate those walls. That person has closed herself to receiving.

Now recognize the perfection of her Being. Be aware of "the smile inside you" as the tenseness in you shifts to relaxation. As the person in front of you takes a breath, she opens to receive and becomes aware of the love within. She becomes aware of your acceptance of who she is and the walls collapse. You have given her the greatest gift of all; you have assisted her in opening to receive the radiance of love from within.

As you continue to visualize, you will begin to feel the radiance of the love as it expands, and your own Being becomes more aware of its perfection. Like a beautiful dance in motion, the more you see the perfection in another, the more you open yourself to receive the radiance of love.

Jesus saw only perfection in all things;

many were healed as they acknowledged the radiance of that Love

It is as though a figure-eight pattern forms between the two of you. As one opens and receives, the waves of radiance expand, allowing the other to open and receive, creating another wave of radiance. You may find yourself swaying back and forth within the energy. Become conscious of the joy (that sense of expansion and light, giggly feeling) building up inside you. When you recognize the perfection of someone else, the love automatically begins to transmute the heavy, distorted energy back into rays of pure light. You feel lighter and in bliss. *Oh, if we could only stay here forever!*

Judgment

What moves us out of this state of being? When we are filled with love, we feel light, empowered, invincible. Is it possible we are finally becoming aware of our true essence? Have we tapped into the power of our soul? Are we beginning to feel the essence of Unconditional Love? What great force could move us out of this beautiful energy?

There is only one force strong enough to separate you from your connection to the Creator — judgment. As you look at situations and conditions around you, you have a choice — watching with interest, or making comparisons. Standing in love, or making judgments.

Love has a vibration that raises the resonance of your Being. Fear, which is a product of judgment, has a vibration that depletes your resonance. As you move into judgment and fear, your Being fills with distorted vibrations and you feel heavy and weak. Your mind takes control and you separate from the essence of your soul.

Remember, the choice is yours; you are in control. You can choose to live in love and joy, or you can choose to live in fear and judgment.

High-level wellness is possible only when we move into a state of nonjudgment and acceptance of the love that we are.

To live a life of nonjudgment is to live a life of eternal health.

Divine

As my thoughts slip back into the past
I find myself
reliving old issues
Stuck
in limbo with no movement forward
my heart aches
in the pain of the judgment
of myself and others

There is no love here
only denial of the Divinity within
judgment is the antichrist of my Being

As I shift my consciousness to the present
and choose to live in a world of nonjudgment
my heart smiles
and the radiance
lifts the shadows of sadness
like fog before sunrise

The eternal flame of Love
lights my way
as I awaken to the Divinity within

Feeling the Presence of Your Angels

by ann marie

The Angels are with us at all times; they assist us in remembering the Divine Love within us. They see us as perfect in every way. They guide and assist us, making our journey easier and more joyful. They embrace us in love, allowing us to remove the resonance of disharmony from our Being.

Have you asked the Angels for help?

Have you hugged an Angel today?

I love to teach people how to perceive their Angels and give them a hug. Allow me to assist you in meeting your Angels.

First you must perceive your own energy field and that of another. As the life-force energy flows through your Being, it emanates outward from the physical body and into your aura. Feel the energy flow in your arm circuit by moving your hands back and forth swiftly, as if you intend to clap them; but do not allow your hands to come together. Holding them apart, slowly bring them toward each other until you feel something between them. You may feel a slight pressure or resistance, a soft breeze, a warmth, or a tingling; it might feel cool, warm, rough, velvety, fluid, etc. Everyone perceives differently. Don't become discouraged if you don't feel anything right away. You are opening up a new area of perception for your computer (brain) to analyze.

As a child, you learned to identify your world through sense perceptions. The frequencies you saw, you identified as different colors. At first you recognized all frequencies within a certain spectrum as blue. Later you were able to become more precise and distinguish between aqua, turquoise, royal blue, navy blue and sky blue. In the same way, the more you practice identifying what you feel, the more you will be able to feel.

Invite others to share these experiences with you.

- ♥ Stand facing them and hold your hands 4 or 5 inches above your partner's hands.

- ♥ Move your hands up and down; feel the energy between you.

- ♥ Feel the smile within your Being as you perceive the love within your partner. (Notice the shift from tension to ease.)

- ♥ Notice how the energy instantly expands between your hands.

- ♥ Face your partner and place your hands about 4 or 5 inches in front of his face.

- ♥ Move your hands downward in front of his body (from the top of the head to the waist), feeling the energy (the aura).

- ♥ Ask him what he perceives as you move your hands in front of his body.

- ♥ Now reverse roles. Stand still while your partner feels the energy in your aura from the top of your head to your waist. You will perceive the energy radiating from his hands.

- ♥ Move away from your partner and ask your Angel to stand in front of you.

- ♥ Hold out your hands and ask the Angel to place its hands above yours.

- ♥ Feel the energy from the Angel's hands. Feel the joy within your Being as you perceive the love of your Angel.

- ♥ Reach out and feel the aura of your Angel. It may be tall or short, masculine or feminine, cute and cuddly or wise and noble. Perceive what you can. (Some people choose to close their eyes so they can focus on the energies.) The more often you do this, the more you will perceive. Many people have told me that after a few days they have become aware of their Angels' names and the role they play in their life.

- ♥ Allow the Angel to feel your aura and be aware of its touch.

- ♥ Ask your Angel to put its arms around you and give you a hug. Be aware of the joy within, and feel the waves of energy between you as you begin to rock in the arms of love. Breathe deeply and allow yourself to be filled with the radiance of love.

Everyone has Angels. Most have several Angels around them at one time. Call forth three Angels to come forward one at a time; feel each one's aura and have each give you a hug. Be aware of the difference in their energies and the feelings they evoke. They will remind you of all that you are and all that you can be.

We were able to capture the effect of receiving a hug from an Angel by means of Kirlian photography. Please see page 86 in the color insert "Auric Photographs."

Have you hugged your Angels today?

Joy

Joy is
love that twinkles
moving you from one situation to another
opening the pathways of discovery
into who you are
and the gifts that you have buried
in the depths of your Being

It rises in the morning
waiting to be greeted
sitting still until acknowledged
It awaits

When overshadowed by other emotions
like the sun behind a large cloud
It awaits

Like an angel wanting to caress you in its wings
and share its radiance
It awaits

Soul-Breathing

As you hugged your Angel, you experienced receiving the radiance of love into your Being. Now let us take this one step further by allowing the individual cells of our body to let down their barriers and receive the love they crave.

Meditation has been used for centuries to raise the resonance of love within the Being and raise the consciousness to accept still more. When we meditate, we focus on love going through our Being. Some of the cells are open to receive; however, the consciousness or mind of many of the cells is closed. The cells are holding their breath, holding their walls of protection in place. It is like sending the light of love through a hose instead of a sponge.

The concept that I use to get the cells to drop their walls and breathe in the radiance of love is called Soul-Breathing.

Soul-Breathing is

The Soul in every Cell

Breathing

the Radiance of Love

To Soul-Breathe,

Feel the embrace of your Angel

(B R E A T H E)

At the same time

Feel the "smile within" you

(notice the shift from tenseness to ease)

(B R E A T H E)

When you feel the smile within (the shift), you acknowledge the radiance of your inner Being. As you take a conscious breath, the cells awaken to receive, allowing your body to regenerate, rejuvenate and reverse the aging process.

If you find yourself unconsciously rocking your body back and forth, the rhythm of your Being has changed. Your breathing may appear to be deeper, and may even feel as though you are breathing from the depths of your pelvis or from outside your body. As you repeatedly Soul-Breathe, you will feel grounded, and at the same time your conscious awareness continues to expand. Using Soul-Breathing allows you to transcend into a new dimension of love, bringing heaven unto Earth through your physical existence.

Harmonic Synchronistic Attunement

When you consciously Soul-Breathe several times a day, your regular breathing will become Soul-Breathing. As your cells open up to receive the radiance of love, you will become aware of the disharmonies within your body. Remember, different parts of your body may have separated themselves with barriers during emotional and physical stress. Each part of the body can be doing its own thing, like the players in an orchestra tuning up before a concert. As long as each instrument does its own thing, the discordance is unnerving. Until the orchestra leader takes control and they begin to play in harmony, you will not be aware of the beautiful music that is possible. As you open each part of your body to receive the radiance of love, it will become attuned to the rhythm of your Being.

You may go through your entire body one part at a time, paying special attention to those parts in the greatest disharmony. I suggest that you begin with the heart. (Breathe until you feel the energy of joy radiating in the heart and expanding throughout your body.)

As you focus on the heart,

Feel the embrace of your Angel
(B R E A T H E)
At the same time
Feel the "smile within" you
(B R E A T H E)
Follow the "smile"
(the shift into relaxation)
as it travels through your body
and joins the radiance of your aura

As the heart takes a breath, the rhythm in the body changes and your whole being feels lighter as distorted frequencies are transmuted in the radiance of love. Using the exercise above, continue to go through the body, focusing on each individual part. You may use the following list.

Collarbone	Hips
Sternum	Sacrum
Breasts	Public bone
Ribs	Thighs
Shoulders	Knees
Upper arms	Calves
Elbows	Ankles
Forearms	Feet
Wrists	Legs
Hands	Chest
Skull and facial bones	Lungs
Brain stem	Abdomen
Spine	Stomach
Tailbone	Lower Abdomen

- ♥ Organs: If you wish, focus on each organ separately, or collectively as a group.

- ♥ Glands: Focusing on the general location of the individual glands is sufficient.

- ♥ Thymus gland: One of the most important, yet the least considered gland in the body; located above the heart and 2 or 3 inches below the base of the throat.

- ♥ Pineal, pituitary and hypothalamus glands: Found near the center of the brain.

- ♥ Thyroid: Located in the neck (throat area).

- ♥ Adrenals: Just above the kidneys on either side of the small of the back.

- ♥ Pancreas: In the abdomen, slightly left of the middle.

- ♥ Ovaries or testes.

A short session of Soul-Breathing can lead to many changes in your body. After a session, walk around and be aware of the adjustments your body has made. Take note of the changes that you are aware of. Does your body feel less dense? Are you standing straighter? Are you walking differently? Does your body feel different in other ways? If you were in pain, has it decreased?

Each part of the body is connected to the whole; what affects one area affects another. When one area takes a breath, others will awaken with it. It is not necessary for you to know anatomy. When you feel the smile (the shift to relaxation), you are opening energy channels and allowing the radiance of love to expand. As you Soul-Breathe, the intelligence of the body takes over and directs the energy where it needs to go. Consciously Soul-Breathing several times a day will do wonders for your total well-being.

Only Love Can Heal

You may desire to focus on certain areas of your body for specific reasons or you may want to know when certain areas of your body put up walls of protection. For this reason we have included the following chart.

ENERGY BARRIER	CAUSE OF BARRIER	DEALS WITH	AFFECTED AREAS OF BODY
Adrenals	The shock of death	Circulation, detoxing, lymph	Hips, glands
Ankles	Fear of life	Stability, enthusiasm for life	Feet, immune system, spleen
Left	Experiencing loss	Overly cautious, fluids	Lymph, connective tissue
Right	Feeling unsafe	Life potential, regeneration, joy	Sinus, hips
Brain stem	Emotional over death	Control centers, flexibility	Tailbone, sternum
Breasts	Not feeling nurtured	Overweight, reproduction	Sinus, lungs, sternum
Calves	Feeling restricted	Elimination, fluid transport	Intestinal tract, colon
Left	Fear of moving	Boundaries, physical restrictions, fluids	Connective tissue, intestines
Right	Disempowered	Weakness, muscle fatigue, detoxing	Muscles, connective tissue
Collarbone	Feeling disempowered	Mineral distribution, hormone balance	Blood, bones
Colon	Feeling of not being wanted	Elimination	Blood, bones
Elbows	Screaming	Cushioning emotional pain, overweight	Diaphragm, lymph
Left	Traumatic blow to the body	Cushioning pain, structural alignment	Connective tissue, skin, CNS*
Right	Acute illness, high fever	Being flexible	Bones
Feet	Disempowered	Vital organs, circulation	Ankles, connective tissue
Forearms	Resisting change	Freedom to move	Joints
Left	Feeling insecure and unsafe	Metabolism and utilization of nutrients	Abdomen, bones
Right	Feeling threatened	Detoxing, reaching out for assistance	Fingers, hands, lymph
Hands	During depression	Ability to receive love	Can affect whole body

*Central nervous system

ENERGY BARRIER	CAUSE OF BARRIER	DEALS WITH	AFFECTED AREAS OF BODY
Heart	Losing the love for life	Energy, body rhythms and patterns	Thymus
Hips	Afraid to move	Movement, stamina	Sacrum, legs, brain stem
Hypothalamus	Sense of being tormented	Weight, blood-sugar regulation	Fatty tissue, liver, thymus
Kidneys	Grief over death	Oxygenation, blood transport, fluids	Heart, lungs
Knees	Frozen in terror	Stability, breathing	Diaphragm, elbows
Left	Weeping	Blood and oxygen transport	Diaphragm, hips, lungs
Right	Trembling	Metabolism, adrenalin	Adrenals, blood vessels, lymph
Liver	Feeling abandoned and alone	Life potential	Heart, lungs
Lungs	Fear of dying	Enthusiasm for life	Heart, ribs, sternum
Pancreas	Shattered emotions	Freedom and letting go	Heart, thymus, glands
Pelvic cradle	When feeling shame	Reproduction, urination, sexual response	Bladder, uterus, prostate
Pubic bone	Emotional distress	Hormone balance, menstruation	Collarbone, uterus, bladder
Ribs	In stress over relationships	Blood and oxygen flow, cardiovascular	Sternum, blood vessels
Sacrum	In fear of something that is terrifying	Flexibility, fluids	Hips, back, sternum
Shoulders	Feeling sorry for self	Body rhythms, strength, accepting self	Collarbone, vertebrae
Left	In panic	Breathing, transfer of oxygen, weight	Lungs, red blood cells
Right	Taking the responsibilities of others	Blood sugar and lipids	Carotid arteries, pancreas, spleen
Shoulder blades	In deep emotional pain	Pivot point of emotional reactions	Connective tissue, sinus, skin
Left	Feeling physical abuse	Digestion and utilization of protein	Stomach, spleen, hair
Right	Feeling hurt	Self-esteem, flexibility, tenacity	Body fluids

ENERGY BARRIER	CAUSE OF BARRIER	DEALS WITH	AFFECTED AREAS OF BODY
Spleen	Pain of rejection	Organization	Immune system, blood
Sternum	First encounter of emotional abuse	Ability to receive love	Heart, liver, abdomen
Stomach	Affected by negativity	Metabolism, utilization of nutrients	Bones, brain, colon
Tailbone	Feeling powerless against intimidation	Fear of unknown, aging, rejuvenation	Sacrum, brain stem
Thighs	Emotional distress	Immune system, joy, strength	Hips, muscles, spleen
Left	Lack of emotional strength	Moving forward	Pubic bone, calves
Right	Frustration	Security, life potential	Ankles, ovaries, male genitals
Thymus	Perceiving that all things die	Weight, life potential, aging	Body regulators
Upper arms	Physically forced against will	Breathing, self-esteem	Ribs, diaphragm, lungs
Left	Betrayed	Reaching out, trusting	Lining of stomach & intestines
Right	When shamed into disempowerment	Reaching out and receiving	Muscles, abdomen
Vertebrae			
Cervical	Feeling hurt	Veins and arteries, oxygen transport	Each cervical, thyroid, pineal
Thoracic	Feeling emotionally weakened	Control centers of the body	Ribs
Lumbar	Feeling the burden of responsibility	Strength, passage of fluids, stamina	Legs, lower back, sacrum
Wrists	Worrying	Moving freely	Face, nerves, l. & r. forearms
Left	Feeling devastated	Energy levels	Right wrist, blood, lymph
Right	Acquiescing to hopelessness	Freedom of hands to manifest desires	Tendons, joints, cartilage

Love Heals

There is nothing more powerful than the word "God." It is the universe. It is the stars. It is love. It is the food that you eat and the air that you breathe. It is every cell in your body, the energy that flows within you. It is the expression of the Creator. It is *you*.

Allow yourself to be who you are. *You* are the Universe of your Being.

When you come to the end of your busy day, reflect on all that you have accomplished, for each day you grow from your experiences. Whether you spent the day at work, playing golf, knitting, going to a play, planting flowers, scrubbing the floor, caring for the children, a trip to the zoo, caring for a friend in need, meditating or in prayer, you have grown. It is all part of your spiritual journey. It is how the soul grows.

No experience is greater or less important than another. Bless your day. Bless your teachers — they are your family, your friends, those with whom you have had a brief encounter. For each has brought you a message; each has interacted with you in your life experience. Take the value of each experience, for it is the foundation on which the soul grows.

✧ ✧ ✧ ✧ ✧

There has been much written about the Healing, but all the words, all the thoughts, all the meanings can be expressed in two words.

Love Heals

The Affirmations

All the affirmations in this book are listed here for your easy reference should you choose to review them from time to time. It would be inappropriate to ask others to read the affirmations if they do not first understand their purpose and intent. Allow them to experience the Healing as you have.

Following each affirmation, take a full, relaxing breath, inhaling through your nose and exhaling through your mouth. Feel the joy radiating from your heart to every part of your Being.

✧　✧　✧　✧　✧

Establishing Intent to Move Forward (pp. 109, 125)

Whatever is interfering with my Free-Will Choice

or my ability to move forward in my life

according to my Heart's Desire,

I now choose to release.

So be it!

✧　✧　✧　✧　✧

If there is anything interfering with your free-will choice, do you choose to be free?

Removing Entities (p. 110)

From the Divine Love that flows through my Being:
Whatever is in my auric field
that is interfering with my Free-Will Choice,
whether it is here with or without my permission,
I now command in the name of the Creator
and from the Divine Love that flows through my Being
in Love and Peace,
that it now go to the Nucleus of its Being.
Go in Peace.
So be it!

✧ ✧ ✧ ✧ ✧

Removing Entities and Clearing Property (p. 115)

I call forth Archangel Michael
to stand at the head of my property,
and Archangel Raphael to stand at the foot.
I ask now that you spread your Golden Wings
and sweep my property of any entities that are interfering
with the Free-Will Choice of myself or my property,
whether they are there with or without my permission.
I ask that they now be removed by you,
taken to the Nucleus of their Being,
never to return.
So be it!

Transmuting Toxic Metals and Toxic Residue (p. 121)

From the Divine Love the flows through my Being:

Surround my Soul with your Divine Light.

Allow now that your Divine Light,

your Light of Love,

your Light of Healing,

your Light of Protection,

your Light of Power and Wisdom,

become a permanent part of every molecule

of the toxic metals in my body

now and throughout my lifetime.

I also include all toxic residues

on all levels of my Being

now and throughout my lifetime,

through all Time and Space and Beyond.

Allow now that they resonate

at the highest frequency of Unconditional Love.

Allow no negative thoughts or harmful energies to enter,

only the purest and the highest.

And no one shall change this affirmation

until I do so of my own Free-Will Choice.

So be it!

✧   ✧   ✧   ✧   ✧

Before a change can take place, you must first make a commitment to change your life:

Declaring My Intent (p. 126)

It is my desire to be Well, Whole and Perfect
in Mind, Body and Soul.

Preparing to Receive Healing (p. 130)

From the Divine Love that flows through my Being:
It is my intent that all Affirmations
I say this day, and each day,
reflect through all Time and Space and Beyond
and on all levels of my Being.
I now call forth the Nucleus of my Being,
the very Core of my Wholeness,
to integrate with me in Unconditional Love,
in Mind, Body and Soul,
to accept this Healing.
So be it!

✧ ✧ ✧ ✧ ✧

Integrating All Aspects of Being (p. 132)

From the Divine Love that flows through my Being:
I call forth all aspects of my Being
that are tethered to the Earth
to stand before me
as I stand before you – in Love.
I ask you now to integrate with me in Unconditional Love.

I call forth all aspects of my Being
to stand before all other aspects of my Being.
I ask you now to forgive all aspects,
to accept forgiveness,
and to release all bonds between you
except that of Unconditional Love.
I ask you to join me now as I embrace you in Love
to move through all time.
I now call forth the fragments of my Being, joyfully united,
to move through all time in Peace and Harmony.
So be it!

✧   ✧   ✧   ✧   ✧

Removing Interfering Energies and the Shadow of Fear
(pp. 137-138, 174)

From the Divine Love that flows through my Being:

Whatever laws I have owned,

whatever beliefs I may hold,

whatever vows I have made,

whatever contracts or agreements I have made

and those I have made them with –

through all Time and Space and Beyond

and on all levels of my Being

that have created these Judgments within my Being

that are not bringing me Happiness and Joy,

Now, of my own Free-Will Choice,

I release.

Goodby and God bless.

I now call forth the Angels of Divine Perfection

to assist me in restoring myself

and my property, past, present and future,

and the Elementals attached to that property,

all to its Divine Perfection.

I call forth the Shadow of Fear,
including all laws, judgments and fears relating to it,
as well as all property that I own, past, present and future,
to stand before me now as I stand before you – in Love.
I ask you now to forgive me as I forgive you.
I thank you for the lessons that we have shared.
I now choose to release all bonds between us
except for those of Unconditional Love.
And I now choose to transmute those laws, judgments,
fears and property into Unconditional Love.
I bid you to go in Peace.
So be it!

✧ ✧ ✧ ✧ ✧

Removing Other Interfering Energies (pp. 110, 142-143)

I call forth Archangel Michael to stand at the head of my Soul
and Archangel Raphael to stand at the foot.
I ask that you spread your Golden Wings
and surround my Soul with Light, Love and Protection.
I ask now:
Anything that is interfering with my Free-Will Choice –
whether it has been placed there with or without my permission,
be it thought forms, monitors, restrictions, bindings,
anything at any level of my Being –
through all Time and Space and Beyond,
Remove it now, take it to a place of your choosing
and dispose of it according to your will, never to return.

I also call forth anything that has been severed or altered
in any form, at any level of my Being,
through all Time and Space and Beyond,
to be reconnected and aligned in Divine Perfection,
for I now choose to be whole.

At this time I ask that the Umbilical Cord of Life

that attaches my Soul to all other Souls now be brought forth,

and any darkness that lies within the Umbilical Cord of Life

also be called forth, to be Loved and Honored,

for it has served me well in my journey.

But I choose to be Well, Whole and Perfect

in Mind, Body and Soul,

And I choose to replace that darkness

with the pure Light of Unconditional Love,

to be enfolded once again into my Being

as I now move forward in my journey.

I thank you, Archangels Michael and Raphael,

for your loving presence.

I bid you to go in Peace, and ask only that you leave with me

the essence of your Love and your Protection

to surround my Soul as I move forward in my journey.

So be it!

✧   ✧   ✧   ✧   ✧

Removing Interfering Relationship Entities (p. 139)

From the Divine Love that flows through my Being:
Whatever is in my auric field
and the auric fields of my relationships –
with individuals, with groups,
with the Earth, with the Universe and with the Creator,
and on all levels of my Being
through all Time and Space and Beyond –
that is interfering with my Free-Will Choice,
whether it is here with or without my permission,
I now command, in the name of the Creator
and from the Lord God of my Being
in Light and Love,
that it now go to the Nucleus of its Being.
Go in Peace.
So be it!

✧   ✧   ✧   ✧   ✧

Releasing Laws and Judgments (Chakra #1)
(pp. 137, 147)

From the Divine Love that flows through my Being:

Whatever laws I have owned,

whatever beliefs I may hold,

whatever vows I have made,

whatever contracts or agreements I have made,

and those I have made them with –

through all Time and Space and Beyond,

and on all levels of my Being –

that have created these Judgments within my Being

that are not bringing me Happiness and Joy,

now of my own Free-Will Choice,

I release.

Goodby and God bless.

So be it!

✧ ✧ ✧ ✧ ✧

Releasing Fears (Chakra #2) (p. 152)

From the Divine Love that flows through my Being:
Whatever fears I may have,
I know I have experienced them before.
And since I have known them before,
I choose not to experience them again.
I now choose to forgive all my fears
and all my reactions to those fears.
So be it!

✦　✦　✦　✦　✦

Reclaiming My Power (Chakra #3) (p. 155)

From the Divine Love that flows through my Being:
I Love and Honor those
who have placed their power over me,
but I now choose
to return their power to them.
I now reclaim my birthright,
and I reclaim my Power,
and I will not relinquish it again.
So be it!

✦　✦　✦　✦　✦

You cannot acknowledge Love for the Creator and deny its Creation in the same breath.

Self-Worth (Chakra #4) (p. 157)

From the Divine Love that flows through my Being:

I declare my values,

my worth.

I am worthy of being Loved

and of Loving others.

Because what you see

is what you get.

So be it!

✧ ✧ ✧ ✧ ✧

Communicating with Being (Chakra #5)

Seeing and Hearing God in All Things (Chakra #6)

The Divinity Within (Chakra #7)

The Three Higher Chakras (p. 158)

From the Divine Love that flows through my Being:
With these lips, I speak God in all things;
with these ears, I hear God in all things;
and with these eyes, I see God in all things.
I now command my Crown Chakra to be open
and bring forth to me those Laws I have owned
through all Time and Space and Beyond
that have created these Judgments
that have not brought me Joy.
Bring them forth before me now
so that I may see them
and release them.
So be it!

✧   ✧   ✧   ✧   ✧

Desires of My Heart (pp. 159)

From the Divine Love that flows through my Being:

I open my Mind, Body and Soul

and ask that you fill my Being,

with your infinite Love,

your infinite Healing,

your infinite Protection,

your infinite Power and Wisdom.

I now call forth my Grand Adventure,

in Feelings and Emotions,

in all things that come in Light and Love,

that will bring me Happiness and Joy.

So be it!

✧ ✧ ✧ ✧ ✧

You may choose to add any specific affirmations that you feel are appropriate for you at this time. If either of the following two affirmations meet your desires at this time, you may choose to use them.

Calling Forth My Prosperity (p. 160)

From the Divine Love that flows through my Being:
I call forth my Abundance and Prosperity
in all forms that will bring me Happiness and Joy.
So be it!

✦ ✦ ✦ ✦ ✦

Calling Forth a Sharer (p. 160)

From the Divine Love that flows through my Being:
I call forth a Sharer,
One who is my equal,
who will grow as I grow,
that we may grow together.
So be it!

✦ ✦ ✦ ✦ ✦

Mind (p. 161)

From the Divine Love that flows through my Being:
I give my Mind permission
to give me Reason and Logic,
but I do not give it permission
to tell me what to do.
So be it!

✦ ✦ ✦ ✦ ✦

Releasing Control Patterns (p. 161)

From the Divine Love that flows through my Being:
whatever Laws that I have owned
regarding my control patterns,
through all Time and Space and Beyond
and on all levels of my Being,
I now choose to release.
So be it!

✦ ✦ ✦ ✦ ✦

Transmuting Thought Forms and Thought Patterns
(p. 162)

From the Divine Love that flows through my Being:

I call forth all my Thought Forms and Thought Patterns –

through all Time and Space and Beyond

and on all levels of my Being –

to stand before me now

as I stand before you – in Love.

I now choose to transmute

my Thought Forms and Thought Patterns

into Unconditional Love.

I now call forth only those Thought Forms and Thought Patterns

that will bring me Joy.

So be it!

✧ ✧ ✧ ✧ ✧

Filling My Being with Love (p. 163)

I now command that all Voids of my Being –

through all Time and Space and Beyond

and on levels of my Being –

now be filled with Unconditional Love.

So be it!

✧ ✧ ✧ ✧ ✧

Transmuting the Shadows of My Being (p. 163)

From the Divine Love that flows through my Being:
I call forth the Shadows of my Being –
on all levels of my Being,
through all Time and Space and Beyond –
to stand before me now
as I stand before you – in Love.
I thank you for the lessons we have shared,
but I now choose to transmute these Shadows
into Unconditional Love.
So be it!

✧ ✧ ✧ ✧ ✧

Releasing Addictions (p. 164)

From the Divine Love that flows through my Being:
I call forth my Addictions to stand before me now.
I thank you for the lessons that we have shared,
but I now choose to release all bonds between us
accept for that of Unconditional Love.
I release these addictions to the Light.
I choose to reclaim my Power,
and I will not relinquish it again.
So be it!

✧ ✧ ✧ ✧ ✧

Releasing Boundaries and Limitations (p. 165)

From the Divine Love that flows through my Being:
All Laws that I have owned
regarding my boundaries and limitations –
through all Time and Space and Beyond
and on all levels of my Being –
I release.
I declare that I have no boundaries and limitations,
and I give myself permission to be all that I AM,
to stand in my Truth
in Unconditional Love,
with no judgment of myself
or of others.
I honor all others for the journey they have chosen,
but I now choose to be the observer
and not a participator,
if that is what I choose in the moment.
So be it!

✧ ✧ ✧ ✧ ✧

Where it calls for [name], include those with whom you have had a close relationship, such as parents, siblings, spouses, relationships (business or personal), children, etc.

Releasing Bonds (p. 167)

From the Divine Love that flows through my Being:
All Souls, Elementals and Thought Forms that I call forth this day,
it is my intent that all aspects of their Souls
and all aspects of my Souls be present,
and that this reflect through all Time and Space and Beyond,
and on all levels of our Being.
I call forth the Nucleus of our Beings,
the Core of our Wholeness,
to participate in this Healing.

From the Divine Love that flows through my Being:
I now call forth [name] to stand before me
as I stand before you – in Love.
I ask now that you forgive me as I forgive you.
I embrace you in Love
and I thank you for the lessons that we have shared,
but I now choose to release to the Light
all bonds between us except that of Unconditional Love.
I bid you to go in Peace.
So be it!

After calling forth those names you desire, conclude with the following:

Forgiveness (pp. 168-169)

From the Divine Love that flows through my Being:
I now call forth all Souls, Elementals and Thought Forms
to stand before me
as I stand before you– in Love.
I ask now that you forgive me as I forgive you.
I embrace you in Love
and I thank you for the lessons that we have shared,
but I now choose to release to the Light
all bonds between us except that of Unconditional Love.
I bid you to go in Peace.
So be it!

I release to the Light at this time
absolutely everything that is not of the Light,
on any dimension,
within any part of my Body, my Mind and my Soul,
within the Nucleus of my Being.
I am at one with God at this time.
So be it!

✧ ✧ ✧ ✧ ✧

Remembering My Creativity and Divinity (p. 169)

From the Divine Love that flows through my Being:
I call forth my Angels to stand before me now,
as I stand before you – in Love.
I ask you now to assist me in remembering
my Creativity and my Divinity.
I ask that you bring this forth
in a manner that will bring Joy to my heart
and a smile to my lips.
I look forward to your presence always.
So be it!

✦ ✦ ✦ ✦ ✦

Aligning the Being in Perfection (p. 166)

From the Divine Love that flows through my Being:
In the name of the Creator
and from the Divine Love that flows through my Being,
I command that every cell in my body
and every vibration of my Being
align itself in Divine Perfection,
for I desire to be all that I AM.
I choose to be all that I AM.
I AM all that I AM.
And I now call forth my Identity in Divine Perfection.
So be it!

Acknowledging My Creation (p. 171)

From the Divine Love that flows through my Being:
I call forth every cell in my body
and every vibration of my Being
to stand before me now,
as I stand before you – in Love.
I acknowledge my Love for you.
I acknowledge the hard work that you have performed for me
to support me in my journey.
And I now choose, and I ask of you
that you align yourself with the Nucleus of my Being
in Divine Perfection and according to my Heart's Desire,
and integrate with me once again in Mind, Body and Soul
as I move forward now in my journey.
So be it!

✧ ✧ ✧ ✧ ✧

To establish new thought patterns, repeat the following affirmation each day for the next twenty-one days.

Establishing New Patterns (p. 172)

From the Divine Love that flows through my Being
and the Nucleus of all that I AM:
I reaffirm the Affirmations supporting my choice
to be Well, Whole and Perfect
in Mind, Body and Soul.
So be it!

If you are in a relationship (either personal, family or business), their distorted energies can interfere with your relationship. You may choose to clear those interfering energies by asking those involved:

"If there is anything interfering with our relationship,
may I say a prayer to clear it?"

If you receive their permission, you may go into your quiet space and silently, or aloud, say the following affirmation on their behalf.

Clearing Relationship Entities (pp. 173-174)

"I now call forth [name] to stand before me,
as I stand before you – in Love.
On your behalf
I offer you this prayer to accept or reject
according to your Free-Will Choice.

From the Divine Love that flows through my Being:
Whatever laws I have owned,
whatever beliefs I may hold,
whatever vows I have made,
whatever contracts or agreements I have made
and those I have made them with –
through all Time and Space and Beyond
and on all levels of my Being –
that have created these Judgments within my Being
that are not bringing me Happiness and Joy,
I now choose to release.
Goodby and God bless.

I now call forth the Angels of Divine Perfection
to assist me in restoring Myself
and my Property, past, present and future,
and the Elementals attached to that property,
all to its Divine Perfection.

I call forth the Shadow of Fear,
including all laws, judgments and fears relating to it,
as well as all property that I own, past, present and future,
to stand before me now,
as I stand before you – in Love.
I ask you now to forgive me as I forgive you.
I thank you for the lessons that we have shared,
but I now choose to release all bonds between us
except for that of Unconditional Love.
I now choose to transmute
those laws, judgments, fears and property
into Unconditional Love.
I bid you to go in peace.
So be it!

Interpreting Auric Colors

There are several interpretations used relating to the colors of the auric field around the body. This is understandable because it is reported that there may be as many as 1000 or more layers to the auric field, and each layer would relate to a different aspect of your Being. I have consulted with a professional therapist who works with auras and can visually see them. The following are her comments.

✧ ✧ ✧ ✧ ✧

There are many factors to be considered when interpreting the aura; therefore the descriptions listed below are general in nature and not intended as a diagnostic tool. The auric photos will show several specific points.

The Heart Center: Varies from mild to intense energy and may reflect a different color than other parts of the aura.

[Reminder: References to left (or right) refer to the colors on your left (while physically sitting down) and not those showing on the photo as you look at it.]

—**Left Side (Future):** The color on your left side is normally the vibration coming into your Being. The closer it is to you, the sooner it will be felt — in a few moments, a few hours, or as long as a few months.

—**Center (Experience):** The color seen over your head is what you experience for yourself now. It is the color that would best describe you. If the color is high, it could mean aspirations, or what you wish to be.

—**Right Side (Expression):** The color on your right side is traditionally the energy being expressed — the vibrational frequency most likely seen or felt by others around you. Many times your friends will think that this is the energy of which you are made. However, it is what you are putting out to the world.

The aura is not necessarily seeing single distinct colors, but rather a combination of shades. Different combinations would be interpreted differently. Here are the colors as seen through the eyes of one therapist.

Red: Intense, powerful emotion; anger; inflammation; physical problems in an active state.

Orange: Reflects emotional more than physical and may reflect sexual arousal. Orange by itself is not considered a problem color, but intermixed with yellow becomes problematic. Intense red-orange is intense passion, not to be confused with pure red, which is problematic.

Yellow: Yellow is not a healthy color. It is the first stage of problematic colors. There are many shades of yellow. The lighter shades are less problematic; the more intense the shade, the more problematic. Yellow can indicate stress and a depletion of your energy. It can also reflect fear or emotional or physical stress.

Violet: A very high spiritual healing energy.

Green: Emerald green is an intense, healthy healing color. However, intermixed with yellow indicates problems still exist. This combination should not be seen as a problem, but rather the problem being resolved, as indicated by the healing energies of green.

Blue: Blue is a very healthy color. The lighter the blue or the more white light that has entered, the greater the movement toward the higher spiritual energies. A darker blue may be interpreted as defensiveness, less openness, a way to protect yourself, but it is not a negative color. Blue of any shade is a positive color.

White: Indicates purity, high levels of spiritual vibrations.

Gold: Not normally seen in this type of photography, but interpreted as someone special who is about to do, is doing, or has done something special of a higher vibration. I mention the color here because I note that some soft pastel yellows may also be seen as a shade of gold. Gold is considered on the same high level as white.

Bright White or Blue Balls of Light: Seen over and to the left of the person, it reflects the clear higher vibrations and the absence of distorted energy patterns.

Translucence: Many auras are so dense that you can barely see the person within the aura. Others (for example, Ann Marie and Rich) have translucent auras. I usually see this only in those who have been taking the Harmonic Vibrational Essences, and so I see this as being on a higher vibrational level. I can tell how long a person has been on the Harmonic Vibrational Essences by the translucence of the aura.

Note: *The aura is not an indicator that one person is more spiritual than another. Everyone is perfect and in the right place on their spiritual journey. The aura is in a continuing state of change according to our emotions and experiences in the moment. It is also a confirmation of the change that has taken place as shown on the photograph.*

Credits and References

Margaret Jackson, photographer (cover photo)
P.O. Box 2023
Sedona, AZ 86339

Golden Seven Plus One by Dr. Samuel West, D.N., N.D., P.M.D.
The International Academy of Lymphology
P.O. Box1051
Orem, UT 84057
1-800-975-0123 / 1-801-226-0123

Hanna Kroeger
7275 Valmont Road
Boulder, CO 80301

Dr. Raymond Noran
1517 Broadway
Hewlett, NY 11557

Vibrational Medicine by Richard Gerber, M.D.
Bear & Company
Santa Fe, NM 87504

Life Between Life by Joe Fisher and Joel Whitney
Doubleday and Company Inc.
245 Park Ave.
New York, NY 10017

Your Body Doesn't Lie by John Diamond, M.D.
Warner Books
P.O. Box 690
New York, NY 10019

Ordering Information

More information is available on the ideas brought forth in

Awaken to the Healer Within.

___ Quarterly newsletter: *Beyond the Healing,* $12.00 year

___ Booklet: *Harmonic Vibrational Essences,* $1.00

___ List of audio and video tapes (send self-addressed stamped envelope)

___ *Awaken to the Healer Within* – $14.95 (3 or more copies less 10%)
      Please include $3.00 s&h for one book, $1.00 per additional book.

Prices shown above are U.S. funds. Outside the U.S.A., please write for rates.

Awaken to the Healer Within is available from your local bookstore.

Name _____

Address _____

City_____ State _____ Zip _____

Date _____ Phone (   ) _____

Send check or money order to:

Asini Publishing
2042 Ryan Road
Mosinee, WI 54455

From the Divine Love that flows through my Being:

Whatever is interfering with my Free-Will Choice

and my ability to move ahead in life

according to my Heart's Desire,

through all Time and Space

and Beyond,

I Release.

So Be It!